LIFE IMPRISONMENT

AN UNOFFICIAL GUIDE

Alan Baker

Life Imprisonment *An Unofficial Guide*
Alan Baker

ISBN 978-1-904380-93-1 (Paperback)
ISBN 978-1-908162-36-6 (Kindle/Epub)
ISBN 978-1-908162-35-9 (Adobe Ebook)

Copyright © 2013 This work is the copyright of Alan Baker. All intellectual property and associated rights are hereby asserted and reserved by the author in full compliance with UK, European and international law. No part of this book may be copied, reproduced, stored in any retrieval system or be transmitted in any form or by any means, including in hard or electronic copy and via the internet, without the prior written permission of the publishers to whom all such rights have been assigned worldwide. The *Foreword* is the copyright of Tim Newell © 2013.

Cover design © 2013 Waterside Press. Design by www.gibgob.com

Cataloguing-In-Publication Data A catalogue record for this book can be obtained from the British Library.

e-book *Life Imprisonment: An Unofficial Guide* is available as an e-book and also to subscribers of Myilibrary, Dawsonera, Ebrary and Ebscohost as well as on Kindle.

Printed by Lightning Source, Milton Keynes.

Main UK distributor Gardners Books, 1 Whittle Drive, Eastbourne, East Sussex, BN23 6QH. Tel: (+44) 01323 521777; sales@gardners.com; www.gardners.com

North American distribution Ingram Book Company, One Ingram Blvd, La Vergne, TN 37086, USA. Tel: (+1) 615 793 5000; inquiry@ingramcontent.com

Published 2013 by
Waterside Press Ltd.
Sherfield Gables
Sherfield-on-Loddon
Hook, Hampshire
United Kingdom RG27 0JG

Telephone +44(0)1256 882250
E-mail enquiries@watersidepress.co.uk
Online catalogue WatersidePress.co.uk

LIFE IMPRISONMENT

AN UNOFFICIAL GUIDE

Alan Baker

Foreword Tim Newell

Winner of a Koestler Award

WATERSIDE PRESS

Contents

Acknowledgements — vii
The Author — ix
Foreword — xiii
Preface — xv
To My Victims — xxiii

1. After Sentence.....................................27
2. Stages of an Indeterminate Sentence 29
3. Tariffs 31
4. Parole — Paper Reviews 33
5. Release from Closed Conditions 35
6. Escorted Town Visits 37
7. Single Cell Occupancy and Relationships................39
8. Prisoners Protesting Their Innocence 43
9. The Offender Assessment System (OASys) 45
10. The Personal Officer Scheme 47
11. Therapeutic Communities 49
12. Making A Contribution..............................53
13. Prison Visits 59
14. Open Conditions 61
15. Release on Temporary Licence (ROTL) 65
16. Lifer Recall 67
17. Driving Lessons 69
18. Travelling Abroad After Release 71
19. Personality Disorder.................................73
20. Prison Politics......................................75

21. Bullying..77
22. Same Sex Relationships..............................79
23. Drugs and Healthcare 81
24. Money Management 85
25. Mental Health Issues..................................87
26. Self-Harm...89
27. Hygiene...91
28. Adjudications 93
29. Artificial Insemination................................95
30. Complaints Procedures 99
31. Access to Official Files..............................103
32. The Criminal Injuries Compensation Authority (CICA)..105
33. Criminal Cases Review Commission (CCRC)..........107
34. The High Court, Court of Appeal, Supreme Court and European Court of Human Rights..................109
35. Offending Behaviour Courses 113
36. Possessions and Volumetric Control 117
37. Tough on Crime, Tough on the Causes of Crime?.........119
38. Bereavement.....................................121
39. Emotional Trauma and Mental Health................123
40. Some Useful Addresses 125
41. Prison Slang 127

Index   129

LIFE IMPRISONMENT

Acknowledgements

Pam Stockwell, for giving me a thirst for knowledge and helping me to discover the good within myself.

Sue-Ann and Michael, for caring.

The violinist, the late-Yehudi Menuhin, for his advice, and for inspiring me to want to make the world a better place for those who need a helping hand.

Virtuoso violinist, Tasmin Little (thank you for the strings.

Ian Pressland, gifted cellist and managing director of the London Chamber Orchestra, and the violinist and teacher at the Royal College of Music, Hilary Sturt—both for their constant encouragement and unwavering support.

Richard Clark (of Clarks Shoes) including for allowing me to play for him.

Lord Hanningfield, for all the interesting conversations we had and treating me like a human being.

Brendan Dowd (former member of the Irish Republican Army) for his words of wisdom that kept me out of trouble on many occasions; and El Masri (ex-Palestinian Liberation Organization) the phonecards and teaching me to weld.

Those prison staff who have gone out of their way to get me closer to release, even when I have let them down; and all the teachers who have helped me to educate myself.

And thanks to others who have helped me over the years: the Reverend Tom Johns (ex-assistant Chaplain General to HM Prison Service); the Reverend Jay Ridley; Elkan Abrahamson;

Allison Leary; Dominic and Dessie Noonan; the late-Charlie McGee; Victor Castagador; the late-Jimmy Robinson (of the Carl Bridgewater Four); Winston Silcott (of the Tottenham Three); Ronnie O'Sullivan senior; Charles Hanson; Eddie Richardson; Jenny Dunbar; Steve Mason; Kim Legget; Eric Leach; the late-artist, Michael Randall; the cellist, Robert Lay; Keith 'Wedge' Thomas (for keeping me entertained); Mitzi Romiti, Savannah and Olivia Ellerby, in Virginia, USA; the billionaire Abbas Gokal, for his financial advice; the gifted guitarist, Tim Nikolai; Charlie Bronson, for cheering me up in the Segregation Unit at Frankland Prison; Johnny 'Chopper John' Kendal; Johnny Dunford; Michelle Saunders; Nicky Dunford, for saving my life; Perry Terroni and Sid Draper; my good friend, Andrew Kennedy; the multi-talented Lynda La Plante, for encouraging me to write; Brian Williamson; Louise and Ajay; Sara and Natasha; Charmaine and Clarissa; Jack and Jay; and Pauline, for her kindness; the staff in Wakefield Prison Segregation Unit for not putting me in one of the cages, even though I deserved it!

Special thanks to the staff at Grendon Underwood (as it was called) therapeutic community, who put up with me for so long, and supported me through one of the darkest periods of my life; and especially to Tim Newell the ex-Governor there for writing the *Foreword* to this book.

Most of all, thank you to my son, William, for giving me a sense of responsibility, purpose, and above all, hope; and my brothers and sisters, their children, and finally my mother who died before I could really get to know her.

The Author

Alan Baker has spent over 20 years in prison (despite a tariff of just nine years) having received a discretionary life-sentence for the attempted murder of another prisoner. He has spent time in some 30 prisons and youth custody centres (as they were known when he was a younger man) and experienced maximum security segregation several times.

Education and training

He has a diploma in drug and alcohol abuse counselling, a certificate in developmental psychology and during his prison 'career' has received training in bricklaying, painting and decorating, industrial laundry, engineering, industrial cleaning, photography, film-making and welding. He also worked as a shepherd at HM Prison North Sea Camp. Information about the courses he has completed is set out at the end of *Section 35*.

Music, Literature and a Koestler Award

The author is an award-winning poet and composer, accomplished violinist and guitarist and a consultant to the London Chamber Orchestra. He has played in over 500 services in prison chapels, performed for the Cheltenham Festival and in Gloucester Cathedral and appeared on BBC local radio. He received a Koestler Trust Silver Award for the manuscript of *Life Imprisonment: An Unofficial Guide*.

The Author of the Foreword

Tim Newell was a Prison Governor for 32 years, ending his Prison Service career as Governor of ground-breaking HM Prison Grendon (with its whole prison therapeutic regime and communities). He was for some years editor of *Prison Service Journal*. His books include *Murderers and Life Imprisonment: Containment, Treatment, Safety and Risk* (with Eric Cullen) and *Restorative Justice in Prisons: A Guide to Making It Happen* (with Kimmett Edgar). He is secretary of Escaping Victimhood[1] a charitable company concerned to ensure that robust support is available to victims of crime once court processes are complete.

---

1 See www.escaping victimhood.com

'When the sentence was concluded, the prisoner acknowledged in a few, scarcely audible words, that he was justly punished, and that he had a fair trial. He was then removed to the prison from which he was never to return.'

Samuel Butler, Erewhon, 1872

'Anyone who is among the living has hope — even a live dog is better off than a dead lion.'

Ecclesiastes 9:4

Foreword

I was recently asked to advise a friend about what to prepare her son to expect when going into prison (as seemed likely at the time). I was not aware of any guidance that was readily available so I made up some suggestions based on my experience of working in prisons, particularly those that received people from court whose first time in custody it was. Sad to say the son was sentenced to custody and I was later reassured that my advice had come to be useful and reassuring. My advice was from a member of staff's perspective inevitably.

If this book had been available and he had got a life-sentence he would have had a fuller view of what to expect and an insider's guide on how to survive and get some benefit from the experience. This is a hard-hitting set of survival notes from someone writing with great experience of having walked the walk. It is grounded in reality, almost painfully too much of it.

Alan Baker writes with sound practical advice and insight which is not for the feint-hearted. He takes prison seriously, recognising it as the last place you want to be. The book is one that staff should read but it may well not be one that they would recommend for although the advice is sound in relation to the experience it does not always express the hope for a balanced, logical approach towards progress through the system. But it will be helpful for prison staff to read it to appreciate the pressures on and priorities of those in custody over long periods of time. The writing is from a person who is a strong prison survivor and well aware of the needs of those who end up in inside.

Alan Baker has spent a long time in prison and there is a wide variety of prisons he spent time in. Through this experience he accumulated much information and has retained an inquiring mind. The range of his experience in prison is impressive and a reflection of how much talent there is within many inside.

He says the words were painful to write and they are painful to read. We do not always appreciate the everyday experience of loss that people in prison live with. Many adapt to survive the daily grind of deprivation. We should never take it for granted that people accept this loss with resignation and are also able to accept responsibility for their past. The growing work using restorative principles and practice is showing the way to work towards this gaining a sense of responsibility.

This book provides a strong testament to the futility of punishment for its own sake and a strong recommendation for ensuring positive learning experiences during prison sentences.

Alan makes a moving apology to the victims he has created through his life and this alone makes his book well worth studying and taking seriously.

Tim Newell
June 2013

Preface

Being in prison is degrading, humiliating and demoralising. For lifers, the effects can be even worse. Long-term imprisonment destroys families, and can lead to prisoners becoming mentally-ill and institutionalised to such an extent that, in some cases, prison becomes less frightening and the prospect of release more so.

The State of the Prisons

Damaged prisoners are still finding it extremely difficult to obtain effective treatment. Many leave prison posing even more of a risk to the public than when first admitted. Prison is often portrayed in the media as a place where inmates relax and enjoy themselves, which leaves victims feeling cheated out of their justice. Restorative justice programmes—those aimed at repairing the harm caused by an offence, to give victims a sense of closure and offenders a chance to see the severe impact their actions have had on their victims, rather than retribution (see further *Section 11* of this book)—are not widely implemented. The Prison Service promises so much, but can deliver so little. It pains me to attack a system which contains many committed and noble men and women, who work tirelessly within our prisons. Some have shared with me their disillusionment, when they see the same prisoners returning time-after-time.

Experiences in Prison

I refuse to look at the past through rose-tinted glasses. I remember vividly the times when I and cell-mates, in a boiling hot cell on a summer's day, had to squat and defecate on an old piece of newspaper, then toss it out of the window, to keep the smell from lingering. We rotted in those cells for 23 hours, every day, for months on end. I remember leaving prison full of hatred, my heart as hard as stone, my self-respect shattered and my dignity destroyed. Imprisonment served only to handicap me, by crushing my confidence, self-esteem and empathy towards others.

Finer feelings are useless commodities in prison, where you are seen as a faceless number in a sea of chaos, fear and dread. I was unable to take responsibility for my own actions when I was so consumed with bitterness, loneliness and despair. I used my anger to prevent myself from self-harming, little knowing how this anger would dull any moral or ethical reasoning within my mind.

The 'Bad Old Days'

In the bad old days, before the Strangeways Riot and subsequent reforms, life was harsh, yet lacked any insight which could have helped me. At the end of the 1980s and in the early-1990s I was overjoyed to see the destruction of the Berlin Wall, Margaret Thatcher kicked out unceremoniously from No.10 Downing Street, and the release of Nelson Mandela. I eagerly awaited dramatic changes within the justice system, but was disappointed to see that prisoners were still being used as political footballs by a succession of Home Secretaries. Prison reforms do not win votes, and every Home Secretary (or since

2008 when responsibility for prisons was transferred, Minster of Justice) feels obliged to be tough on crime. After all, this is what they think the public wants.

Prison is not the same as it was 25 years ago. The days of slopping out may be over, since the widespread introduction of in-cell sanitation, but more — much more — needs to be done to build self-esteem in prisoners, which is, I believe, the only way they will make more positive choices in their damaged lives.

If you take a dysfunctional person from a dysfunctional family and put him in what in my experience sometimes seems to be a dysfunctional institution, the result is easy to predict!

For many prisoners, the road to hell really has been paved with the good intentions of those who support imprisoning more people per head than any other country in Western Europe.

Change, Privileges — and Progress?
Admittedly, many changes have been made within our jails, but still I struggle to equate increased privileges with real progress. Prisoner-on-prisoner violence appears to have increased over the last ten years, and much of this is undoubtedly due to the large number of prisoners using drugs. Acts of violence go unpunished, because prisoners are afraid to testify against other inmates, and an increasing number of non-sex offenders are requesting to be placed in vulnerable prisoner units.

It would appear that a large number of prisoners subscribe to the idea that the more aggressively you act, the more respect you will gain. It is no surprise that these hotbeds of discontent produce nothing but a continuous supply of bodies that must be locked away. It would be too easy for me to say that prisoners are products of their environment, and absolve criminals of all responsibility for their actions. I accept that issues affecting them are more complex and that a multi-faceted approach is needed, if they are to stand a chance of staying out of prison after discharge.

I fear that in the 21st century, prisoners are becoming more feral as a whole and feel nothing for anyone but themselves. Maybe this is a symptom of living in a culture where what you have is more important than who you are?

It is an easy option for the courts to impose indeterminate sentences and hide people away, making the public feel safer; but I would welcome more creative sentencing policies to help free up places in an overburdened penal system.

Overcoming Problems
In spite of the great number of problems faced by prisoners, it is encouraging that many do manage to overcome them and go on to lead constructive lives after release. I applaud all the boys, girls, men and women within our penal institutions who struggle to educate themselves, as it is difficult to be positive when you are being held against your will!

However, if the prison population continues to escalate and funding is not made available to provide adequate services, we will end up with prisons full of idle, uneducated, feckless and unreleasable people. Until we start to treat some of the most vulnerable and damaged members of our community in a more humane manner, we will continue to allow our justice system to be what it has always been, 'an expensive way of making bad people worse'!

Lifer Management

Progress for lifers has always been slow, Parole Boards have always in my experience sat late, prison authorities have always complained about a lack of staff, and there have never been enough places on offending behaviour courses. Although every lifer's situation is unique, they will all experience times of frustration, due to a lack of information. I hope to provide advice that is practical, but, most of all, realistic. Nothing ever happens in prison as it should, especially for lifers, and I feel that it is their right to be made aware of this. Hopefully, this will help them deal with disappointment: prevent them from giving up.

The prison system struggles to manage lifers at present and lacks a truly effective strategy for dealing with those who are scarred by their experiences or traumatised by the crimes they may — or may not — have committed. The general view is that everybody in prison is guilty and that they should accept their punishment without complaint. Although much has changed within the prison system over the last 20 years, unfortunately not all of these changes have been positive ones, as the average time a lifer will spend in prison increases with each year that passes. Hopefully, things will get better in the future and a more humane system will be created for all in prison.

As readers can see, this is not intended as an objective account of how life-sentences work. It would be impossible to be entirely objective, after sometimes living in rundown, under-staffed and to my mind questionably managed institutions for so long. Prison can be a terrifying place, even for a short-term prisoner. For a lifer, it can be soul-destroying and as corrosive as acid. Prisons house the most damaged, dangerous, mentally-unstable, immature, unloved and unwanted members of society, and it is a terrible thing to be locked away among such people, with no idea when, or if, you will ever be released.

I am ashamed that not only have I personally created many victims (see the next section), but appalled that the justice system is creating still more.

The Purpose of this Book

This brief, unofficial guide has been put together to give life-sentence and IPP (imprisonment for public protection) prisoners and other people who may be interested some idea of what is involved. Apart from general information, it appears there is nothing available specifically on the subject of lifers, focusing on the real-life issues that they may face day-to-day. There is certainly nothing written by a lifer. Having spent well over 20 years serving a life-sentence in all categories of prison I hope that a few insights will prove useful.

Some Further Preliminary Thoughts

At the drop of a hat, we can all profess to be moral and ethical people, yet if we were under surveillance for 24 hours a day, any observer would be likely to see how, in our everyday lives, we often put self-interest before the welfare of others. This is perhaps a natural instinct.

Many of us commit crime, from the office worker who nicks a few staples to the home-owner who over-inflates the value of their lost items when making an insurance claim. It is all a matter of degree. The world would be a terrible place to live in if we were all left to our own consciences in deciding what we would or wouldn't do. This is why we have laws to protect us, not only from others, but from ourselves.

Although society may consider itself to be civilised, our history has many examples to show how thin the veneer of civilisation really is. If society's humanity can be measured by how it treats its prisoners, then we have difficult times ahead. Understaffing and underfunding is likely to pose a serious threat to those who believe that constructive and imaginative rehabilitation is the way forward in the fight against crime. Until this issue is resolved, the large and rising number of life-sentenced prisoners will continue to escalate.

As a lifer representative for over seven years, my role was to provide answers to any questions that a lifer might ask. If I had no answer, I would be expected to point the prisoner in a direction where the answer could be found. Unless prison officers are trained specifically to deal with life-sentence issues, they cannot be expected to provide accurate and up-to-date information regarding the many, sometimes complicated, issues which are unique to such prisoners.

Things change all the time: the information in this book can only be a guide and readers, once pointed in the right direction, should always consult the latest HM Prison Service policy, guidance and rules; much of is to be found in Prison Service Orders (PSOs) or the latest Prison Service Instructions (PSIs) (and for prisoners in the prison library). Another source of information, especially concerning the regimes at individual prison establishments, is the website of *Inside Time*, the newspaper for prisons and prisoners, especially under the headings 'Regimes' and 'Inside Information'.[2]

---

[2] See www.insidetime.org

Personal Views and Opinions

Finally, all the opinions expressed in this book are my own and based on my personal experiences inside prison. I am aware that they may not be shared by everyone, but have tried to balance things and hope that no-one, staff or other prisoners alike will take offence concerning what I set out with the best of intentions: helping others.

I should also stress that the choice of contents as they appear in the 40 sections which follow is also a personal matter; in effect a list of topics each with the kind of explanation that I hope will be of use to lifers—and those who would like to now a little more about what it is like to be on a life-sentence.

Alan Baker

A1801AF
June 2013

ALAN BAKER

To My Victims

I wish to take this opportunity to say sorry to all the victims I have created over the years. I am deeply sorry and ashamed for the selfish, thoughtless way in which I behaved, and hope that my victims may one day forgive me. I am aware of the pain that I made them feel and I understand that, even though many, many years have passed, much of the pain still remains.

I could tell you of my childhood and how badly I have been treated by those whose responsibility it was to care for me. You may not care what abuse was inflicted upon me in two children's homes, because I turned my anger on you and made you suffer, too. My life has been one of fear, despair and hopelessness.

The only way I could feel better about myself was when I hurt others. My shame will always live with me and I am haunted by the faces of those who will always hate me. With all my heart, I wish I could undo all the damage I have done to those who did not in any way deserve it.

I was finally sentenced to life imprisonment for trying to murder a fellow prisoner who had been bullying me, and it was then that I realised the kind of fear that my victims must have felt. When the life-sentence was passed, I fainted in the dock. During the last 20 years of my sentence, I have been committed to changing my life by completing numerous offending behaviour courses and learning skills that will enable me to find a job if ever I am released. I am a guilty man and take full responsibility for my actions.

As I explained in the *Preface* to this book, it has been said that prison is an expensive way of making bad people worse. I'm sure that this may be the case for many prisoners, but not me. With the constant love from friends and family members, I have been dedicated in my endeavours to transform myself into a man of worth, who will one day make a positive contribution to society.

My life-sentence has been a most painful experience. Prison is a terrible place to be. It is often a place full of dangerous people, devoid of all humanity, who view each other as potential prey. Yet I have always felt that I deserved every bad thing that has happened to me. I am not proud of the things I did as a teenager, but to survive a life-sentence, I have had to stay focused on the future, and the good within myself. This is difficult after being on some of the most dangerous landings, on some of the most terrifying wings, in some of the most dreadful prisons in Britain.

I have witnessed eight men being slashed with razor blades fixed into toothbrushes as handles, 12 stabbings, three scaldings with boiling hot oil and five with boiling water. I have even been scalded myself. I have known four men who hanged themselves with torn-up bed sheets, and two others who have committed suicide by overdosing.

My own 17-year-old brother was murdered in 1994, so I do know how it feels to be a victim.

I hope my own victims will feel that they have got the justice they deserve and that I received the punishment I deserved. I am not now the person I once was. Prison has not changed me into a perfect human being. My experiences mean that I do think that the prison system cannot reach that level, whether with me or anyone else.

Only love, kindness and understanding can change men's hearts. Prison can make people mean, ruthless, callous and bitter. I hope I have not become one of those people. I ask no sympathy of anyone; I only wish for the forgiveness of those who still think ill of me. I am sorry, remorseful and feel an immense sense of empathy towards those I have hurt.

As I continue to serve my sentence, I can only express my hope that my victims' pain will one day diminish and that the retribution they may still seek will be tempered with compassion.

Alan Baker
June 2013

1 After Sentence

After you receive your sentence, your prisoner category will be decided (see below) and you will usually, at first, be returned to the prison where you spent your remand time. Exceptions to this are when it has been decided that you should be awarded Category-A status. You will then be transferred to a local (allocation) prison able to house Category-A prisoners.

On the day that you get your life-sentence it is normal to feel a variety of different emotions. Shock, despair, anger, confusion, shame and remorse are not uncommon. Any of these emotions, singly or together, could lead to depression without adequate support. The prison healthcare arrangements will be familiar with how you are feeling and are trained to give you support and treatment, if necessary, to assist you through this difficult stage of your sentence.

Listeners (prisoners trained by the Samaritans) are also available to provide support to those in distress. If you feel that you need this kind of support, ask prison staff for a Listener.

You may be feeling that you have let yourself, and/or your family down. This is normal, and it is healthy to acknowledge these feelings. However, at this stage of your sentence, you need to focus on your immediate needs, as you begin to plan how, and where, you will complete your sentence.

You may remain in your local or allocation prison for some months, before it is decided where you will be transferred to serve the first stage of your sentence. This move will depend on two things:

- your prisoner category (below); and

- the offending behaviour courses that it is felt you need to complete (there are references to such courses throughout this book, see especially *Section 35*, and also your sentence plan).

Prisoner Categories: A Short Note

Category A: Those whose escape would be highly dangerous to the public or national security. Offences that may result in consideration for Category A include: murder, attempted murder, manslaughter, wounding, rape, robbery, firearms offences, importing or supplying Class A drugs, terrorism and those under the Official Secrets Act.

Category B: Those who do not require maximum security, but for whom escape needs to be made very difficult.

Category C: Those who cannot be trusted in open conditions but who are unlikely to try to escape.

Category D: Those who can be reasonably trusted not to try to escape, and are given the privilege of an open prison.

The Incentives and Earned Privileges Scheme (IEPS)

The IEPS determines which prisoners enjoy privileges such as additional visits, jobs that earn money, or extra money, in-cell TV, etc. There are three levels: Basic, Standard and Enhanced; each giving different benefits. Prisoners start on Standard Level and gain or lose status based on their progress and behaviour inside prison (see also *Section 28*). There are government moves against progression simply for 'staying out of trouble'.

2 Stages of an Indeterminate Sentence

A life-sentence is made up of a number of stages.

- **Stage 1** This is when you are first allocated to a prison (other than a local prison) to serve your sentence. A sentence plan will be put together, which should take into consideration any offending behaviour courses that you need to complete in order to lower your risk, together with any mental health issues, and any educational needs that you may have. This first stage usually lasts a few years and is dependent on the length of your tariff.

- **Stage 2** During this stage you would be expected to have addressed your offending behaviour, improved your educational and vocational (work) skills and progressed to a Category-C prison. At this stage, a prisoner should hopefully have received some recommendations that they be transferred to an open (Category D) prison to complete the final stage of their sentence. The recommendations most valued by the Parole Board are those from the prisoner's offender manager and psychologist.

- **Stage 3** The prisoner at this stage will be in a Category-D prison (or a Category-D resettlement prison), the difference being that a Category-D prison holds those not deemed dangerous enough to be housed in a closed prison, but who are not yet necessarily safe to be released, whilst at a Category-D resettlement prison, such as Blantyre House, the emphasis is on resettlement back into society. Some prisoners have been held in Category-D prisons for many years. Some are too old or too ill to be tested in work placements in the community (which is what happens at resettlement prisons), while others are disabled and unable to find a hostel placement which is able to provide for their needs or licence requirements. In an ideal world, you will have completed this final stage before your tariff (see next section) date expires, and you look forward to your release.

3 Tariffs

Although some life-sentenced prisoners may have their tariff date set in open court, others may have to wait, possibly for up to a year. Either way the tariff is nowadays set by the trial judge (it used to be set by the Secretary of State). It is important to realise that this tariff date is in no way a release date. If you had received a determinate sentence instead of a life-sentence (or imprisonment for public protection (IPP)[1]) that determinate sentence would be similar to the length of the tariff.

The tariff is the punishment part of the life-sentence. If it is considered that you no longer pose a risk to the public, it is possible, but unlikely, that you could be released soon after your tariff date. If you receive a tariff date of, say, five years and have been recommended to complete offending behaviour courses which are offered in different prisons, you could serve well over your tariff date, just waiting for a place on a course. Unfortunately, the waiting lists are always long, so the sooner you put your name down for one, the better.

Not only is it important to complete as many courses as possible before your tariff date, but you must also fully engage in these courses, be an active participant and complete the 'homework' satisfactorily, before moving on to do another course.

Prisoners can challenge the length of their tariff by contacting

---

[1] In respect of those prisoners to whom this sentence still applies. There are prisoners whose offences occurred before abolition who are still serving, or who may yet still receive this variety of indeterminate sentence.

a solicitor and submitting an appeal to the Secretary of State. Few prisoners have their life tariff reduced, since the Secretary of State is likely to support the decision made by the trial judge. It is possible for a prisoner to challenge a refusal to reduce the tariff once set, if he believes it is too high. Again, he should contact a solicitor as soon as possible.

The Whole Life Tariff
There are a number of life-sentenced prisoners with a whole life tariff. This means that the Parole Board or the Secretary of State for Justice will never consider them for release. Although a whole life tariff is usually given to people who have committed extremely serious or heinous crimes (I think that there may be others who have committed equally serious crimes which might have justified a whole life tariff, yet did not receive one).

The amount of press coverage given to the crime can play a massive part when the prisoner's tariff is decided. This could be seen as unfair. Two people may commit seemingly identical crimes, yet the offender whose crime attracts more media coverage will usually receive a longer tariff than the one whose case went relatively unreported.

A number of whole life prisoners have been trying to challenge their tariff in the European Court of Human Rights, in the hope that pressure will be put on the UK justice system to scrap whole life tariffs and give all lifers the chance to be at least considered for release, if or when it is eventually deemed safe for them to be released.

4. Parole — Paper Reviews

There was a time when a prisoner serving an indeterminate sentence (life or IPP)[2] actually got to see the Parole Board (i.e. one of its panels) when their parole date arrived. It appears that nowadays a *paper* review is often held, where the prisoner does not get to put their case to the Parole Board in person. If you think that you may have a paper review, ensure that your solicitor forwards all information on the progress you have made to the Parole Board secretariat, so that they have all relevant information on which to base their decision.

Forward all positive reports that you may have received, copies of all offending behaviour certificates and reports that you have in your possession, and send in your own written representations. Do not take it for granted that they have copies of any paperwork you may have. Do not sit back and wait — be proactive! Parole Boards do not come around very often for lifers, so do all you can to ensure the best possible result.

Paper reviews have been introduced because of the growing number of prisoners on indeterminate sentences and the small number of Parole Board members. This obviously puts the prisoner at a disadvantage, as the Parole Board will be unable to see them as a human being, only as a name on a piece of paper.

If you feel that the decision of the Parole Board was unfair, you can always apply, via your solicitor, for your case to be

---

2   Again, all references in this book to imprisonment for public protection (IPP) should be understood in the light that this sentence has been abolished: see Footnote 1.

examined by way of judicial review. In some cases, the threat of this is enough for the decision to be overturned.

If the Parole Board makes any recommendation other than release, it is up to the Ministry of Justice to decide whether to accept that recommendation. If they refuse, you can also challenge that decision via judicial review. However, you must be able to prove or demonstrate that the decision of the Ministry of Justice was unfair.

For information about the recall of lifers granted parole, see *Section 16* of this book.

5 Release from Closed Conditions

From the first day in prison, a main focus of every prisoner is on his or her eventual release. Although, technically, it is possible for a lifer to be released from closed conditions, this is highly unlikely (as is also the case for a prisoner serving any kind of indeterminate sentence). The Parole Board and the prisoner's offender manager will usually require the prisoner to be 'tested' in open conditions. After many years in prison, it is felt to be in the best interests of the public, as well as the lifer himself or herself, that long-term prisoners should be eased back into society, rather than discharged with no experience of life outside or no support.

So if you are a lifer, once you arrive in open conditions, it will be the prison's job to decide whether to enter you into its resettlement programme, e.g. working on the outside and returning to prison overnight, or first require you to complete more offending behaviour work. It is possible that you may even be transferred back to a closed prison to complete any courses that are not available in the open establishment.

Monitoring and Observation
Make no mistake, your behaviour will be closely observed and monitored from the moment you arrive in prison. It is in your best interests to take an active part in the prison's community life and avoid associating with antisocial prisoners or drug users. You will be judged by staff, not just on who you are,

but by the company you keep. You do not necessarily have to break any rules to be sent back to closed conditions. You can be returned if staff feel concerned about your behaviour, especially if that behaviour could make you a risk to the public.

You may be fortunate and receive a warning, telling you to focus on the reasons why you are in an open, Category-D prison. Many others will receive no warning whatsoever, especially if it is feared that a warning may cause the prisoner to abscond (e.g. not return to prison after a period of leave for outside work or for an approved outside visit: see also the next section).

You will only be released once you can prove that you present a manageable risk to the public. Of course, this will be an uphill struggle for any lifer. It is not for the Parole Board to prove that you are dangerous. It is for you to prove that you are not.

Although they are supposed to order your release unless you pose a risk to 'the life or limb' of a member of the public, you could be refused parole if you fail a drugs test. The accepted theory is that if you cannot obey small rules, how can you possibly be expected to obey big ones?

Fear of the Outside

It is not unknown for lifers close to release to sabotage their chances by breaking prison rules because they cannot face the idea of freedom and the need to make their own decisions. You should speak to your offender manager if you feel you cannot face the challenge of life outside. He or she will help you to try and overcome those feelings. It is normal to feel afraid or anxious that you may not cope, after many years in prison.

⑥ Escorted Town Visits

Lifers in Category-C prisons can submit an application for an escorted town visit with a member of staff. The purpose is to see if the prisoner will be able to handle the openness and freedom of the outside world, before being transferred to a Category D open prison.

Institutionalised prisoners may normally only apply for one escorted visit each year, as long as they are in a Category-C prison. But these visits are not a right, and often depend on the availability of staff who have time to accompany the prisoner.

There are references to town visits—both escorted and unescorted—in other sections of this book in relation to situations in which the opportunity for such a visit may arise.

LIFE IMPRISONMENT

7 Single Cell Occupancy and Relationships

While, in most cases, staff will try to place long-term prisoners in single cells, unless you are classified as a 'high risk' prisoner, you have no automatic right to a single cell. The only prisoners entitled to a single cell, apart from those deemed high risk, are those who need to be in a one for medical reasons.

Although, from a prisoner's point of view, it is preferable to have a single cell, there can be possible disadvantages. There is a view that spending too much time alone in a single cell can lead to prisoners becoming isolated to such an extent that they start to lose the social skills that develop from sharing a cell. These social skills are needed, especially when a prisoner has to share a cell after spending years in a single cell, and needs to avoid getting into conflict situations with their new cell-mate(s).

They are also necessary when the prisoner reaches the end of his or her sentence, and has to interact with their family and the general public. For some prisoners, relationships and the skills needed to maintain them are not seen as a priority. These skills, however, are what is needed to help a prisoner interact with other prisoners and staff in a pro-social manner.

When deciding whether to release you, or recommend transfer to a less secure environment, the Parole Board will be very interested in how you get on with other people and how you react in stressful situations.

Maintaining Relationship Skills

Maintaining your relationship skills (and strengthening them by completing offending behaviour courses: see also the *Appendix*) will also play an important part in preventing long-term prisoners from becoming institutionalised.

If a prisoner *demands* a single cell, he will usually achieve nothing, except a negative entry in his prison file!

It is vitally important that prisoners try to foster good and positive relationships with all members of staff that they come into contact with. They should, upon arriving on a prison wing, find out the name of their allocated personal officer. His or her job, broadly speaking, is to help a prisoner to achieve the targets set out in their sentence plan. The officer will not only complete progress reports, but will also help, e.g. with appropriate applications and give advice on social issues, such as family problems Any immediate concerns that a prisoner may have regarding their imprisonment or safety should be brought to the personal officer's attention as soon as possible.

A prisoner's ability to demonstrate respectful behaviour towards staff will go a long way towards helping them progress through the prison system as quickly as possible. A prisoner who wishes to get a job in a position of trust will be expected to behave in an adult manner and show the staff that they are stable and present less of a management problem than some of the more needy prisoners who take up much of the staff's time.

In an ideal world, all prisoner and staff relationships would be rewarding and fruitful experiences. It would, however, be true to say that these relationships sometimes leave a lot to be desired. As in any relationship, breakdowns occur, and who is responsible is not always easy to ascertain. Any relationship is a two-way thing, and both parties need to keep an open and non-judgemental attitude, whenever they meet. It is in the best interests of both the prisoner and the member of staff to work at a relationship. It would be helpful to remember, when dealing with members of prison staff, that they are human beings and not miracle workers. Their individual power is limited and just because they are unable to meet a prisoner's demands does not mean that they do not care. Being respectful does not mean being overly familiar. All prisoners and staff within the prison system are expected to act in a professional and mature way, acknowledging social boundaries.

Asking for Help
It is quite difficult for some prisoners to ask anyone for help, especially members of prison staff. When a prisoner does approach a prison officer for help, ideally, as trivial as the subject matter may appear to be, the officer should treat the subject respectfully. Even a small problem that is easily solvable can be the most important thing in a prisoner's mind, especially when they have been in prison for a long time and after they have spent ages in their cell dwelling on it.

LIFE IMPRISONMENT

8 Prisoners Protesting Their Innocence

Technically, there are no innocent men or women in prison. The justice system works on the premise that if someone pleads guilty or is found guilty by a jury, then guilty they must be! Any prisoner protesting his or her innocence will always be viewed as being in denial.

In some cases, a lifer especially may have committed a crime which is so serious that he or she is unable to admit to himself or herself that he or she is indeed guilty. This may simply be a form of 'denial', or they could be overwhelmed with shame, remorse or embarrassment, and would not like their families or friends to even begin to think that they are guilty.

Some prisoners, especially those with an extensive criminal history, plead guilty to crimes they have not committed, because they are likely to receive a lesser sentence than if they had stood trial and been found guilty by a jury. Currently, many may have their sentence reduced by a third if they plead guilty. In such cases, the view of the justice system is that only a guilty person would plead guilty, and if someone pleads guilty to an offence they did not commit, there is little that can be done.

Nobody knows how many prisoners in British jails are really innocent and victims of a miscarriage of justice; but many life-sentenced prisoners have had their convictions quashed by the Court of Appeal.

Almost all lifers who are protesting their innocence will

probably spend most of their lives behind bars. This is because they will be unable to attend offending behaviour courses, and will therefore receive negative reports from their offender managers.

Psychologists always presume that a prisoner is guilty, so that anyone claiming to be innocent will have great difficulty in progressing through a system that is designed for the guilty.

Apart from constantly challenging their convictions through the court system, there is little that these prisoners can do, except complete any offending behaviour courses that are not focused on the actual offence, such as Controlling Anger and Learning to Manage It (CALM), or Enhanced Thinking Skills (ETS).

⑨ The Offender Assessment System (OASys)

OASys is an IT-based offender assessment tool, developed jointly by the Prison Service and Probation Services. It is a tool that offender managers use to predict risk to the public. As a prisoner, this will cover your life in detail from childhood to the present day. It is a comprehensive record of your criminal history, as well as your education and work history.

From the information supplied, your offender manager will use the OASys programme to predict whether you pose a low, medium or high risk to the public. He or she should inform you what offending behaviour work you need to complete to lower your risk.

Risk Assessment

Both your *static* and your *dynamic* risk will be assessed. If you have committed a serious, violent crime, your static risk will usually be high, and it is unlikely to change, since it is based on your criminal history. However, completing offending behaviour courses is an indication that you are developing skills to manage your behaviour in the future. This, hopefully, should result in a reduction of your dynamic risk to medium or low.

Unlike your static risk, your dynamic risk can become lower, or increase, should you commit further crimes, if you are recalled to prison after release, or if you demonstrate behaviour that would be a cause for concern to your offender manager.

It is important that you keep your offender manager up-to-date on the courses that you have completed, your educational achievements, and any voluntary work you may have undertaken, such as participating in the Listeners/Insiders schemes or becoming a Violence Reduction Wing Representative: see *Section 12*.

Your offender manager can then keep your OASys records up-to-date, and so further reduce your dynamic risk.

10 The Personal Officer Scheme

If a prison is running a Personal Officer Scheme, it is essential that the lifer makes contact with his or her personal officer as soon as possible. The lifer will be dependent upon the personal officer for regular reports, and this officer will be the first port of call if the lifer has a problem or needs to apply to attend an offending behaviour course.

The officer will be expected to liaise between the lifer and the Offender Management Unit (OMU) and be aware of any educational/vocational work that the lifer may have completed. It is very important that the lifer tries to get along with their personal officer, as the Parole Board will see all reports that they submit, both good and bad.

If a lifer in a Category-C prison is granted an escorted town visit (see *Section 6*), to help prepare them for the eventual transition to open conditions, their personal officer is usually the one who will be escorting them.

Some personal officers are better at their job than others. If a lifer is not happy with a personal officer who, e.g., may not have submitted necessary reports on time, they may ask for a new one, but (as ever) that could result in a negative entry in the lifer's prison record.

The alternative is for the lifer to become proactive and approach their offender manager to request the reports, rather than directly and personally pressuring the officer concerned.

LIFE IMPRISONMENT

11 Therapeutic Communities

There are a number of prisons which have a wing set aside as a therapeutic community (TC). Prisoners in these communities will be expected to spend about two years challenging and changing the thought patterns which caused them to commit their crimes. They can expect to have their day-to-day behaviour examined and to be held to account by other members of the community.

This could be problematic for some prisoners, as changing any pattern of behaviour is very difficult. It may involve looking deeply into their childhood and the way in which they were treated by their parents. Such prisoners will necessarily make themselves vulnerable, as they reveal painful experiences that they may have lived through. In this way, it is hoped that they will be able to embrace and acknowledge their inner potential for good.

Prisons Specialising in Therapy
Grendon Prison (formerly Grendon Underwood) is a TC based in Buckinghamshire. It is still a prison, but each wing has is its own community. An increasing number of prisoners at Grendon are serving life-sentences. The establishment takes men who are seeking to change their lives, including those who have been damaged and traumatised by their upbringing and the TC approach helps them to deconstruct their belief systems, using group therapy, art therapy and psychodrama,

until the prisoners start to question for themselves their own morality, ethics and so on.

Unlike the situation in some TCs, a prisoner may be at Grendon for an unspecified length of time. Once they are able to demonstrate that they can function in a pro-social manner, they will be transferred back into the general prison system to complete further offending behaviour courses.

No lifers are released from Grendon, as it is a Category-B prison, and most lifers will only be released from an open prison. It is claimed that by spending time engaged in the therapy that Grendon offers, a prisoner will reduce his risk of reoffending. However, the statistics that are put forward to validate this claim were compiled when Grendon was full of prisoners serving determinate sentences. With a larger proportion of inmates (or 'residents' as they are called rather than 'prisoners' or 'inmates') now being lifers, the character of the establishment has changed and not all prisoners benefit from the therapy as they did in the past.

Since 2003, a therapeutic regime at Dovegate Prison has operated under the private sector and differs from the ground-breaking work at Grendon under the Prison Service since the 1960s. Grendon and Dovegate are sometimes described as 'whole prison' therapeutic communities (although as noted Grendon has separate wing communities, whilst a one 'half' of Dovegate is a normal prison). Prisoners thinking of applying to either Grendon or Dovegate can obtain further information on request from those establishments.

Anyone considering a transfer to a TC should be aware that it will not be easy. Some prisoners believe that it will get them out of prison sooner than if they stay in the normal prison system. They could be mistaken. Prisoners can spend many years in a TC, as, understandably, can take years of therapy to undo antisocial and dysfunctional behaviour patterns.

Some prisoners will opt to apply to HMP Dovegate instead of HMP Grendon, as the programme at the former only lasts for two years. To get any benefit from these communities, a prisoner must be willing to examine all aspects of their life with a fine toothcomb. No stone will be left unturned during therapy. No subject is taboo and any secrets will be revealed. Criminality, sexuality and all types of human behaviour will be explored, as you go on the journey to find the real you!

It is advisable for anyone thinking of going to a TC to read about them first,[3] before submitting an application. There is a view that people who leave therapy half-way through a programme will have increased their risk of reoffending, especially in the eyes of the Parole Board.

---

3   For detailed accounts, see *Grendon Tales* (2001), Smartt, U; and *Dovegate* (2011), Cullen E and Mackenzie, J, both from Waterside Press.

LIFE IMPRISONMENT

12 Making A Contribution

For prisoners with the inclination to do so, which should be encouraged, there are jobs you can do within the prison that can make use of your time and talents. If you are a person who wishes to make a positive contribution, to help others who need support and be a role model, you should enquire to see what schemes your prison runs.

By speaking to your wing staff and other inmates, you will be able to do some research into available schemes and what they entail. The primary function of these schemes is to provide a valuable service to the other prisoners who live with you. You will need to be a mature person who can be trusted to focus on the needs of others.

Joining one of these schemes can be a boost to your confidence and self-esteem. You will also be able to develop your communication skills, and report-writers will see you as a proactive member of the prison community. The Parole Board will be interested not only in your attitude towards your crime, and how you have lowered your risk to the public, but also how you have spent your time in prison and how you engage with others. Examples of these schemes follows below.

Listeners
These are unpaid volunteers who are trained and operate under the Samaritans, providing confidential emotional support to other prisoners. Because it is confidential, details will not be

passed on to prison staff unless the person they are supporting gives their permission.

Prisoner Consultative Committee

This is a forum attended by members of staff and prisoners who have been chosen to represent the views of prisoners. These meetings are held regularly and their main purpose is that of communication between staff and prisoners. It is also an opportunity for both parties to air their views and concerns regarding how a wing is being run. Staff can also gain insight into how receptive prisoners are to the policies and rules that they have to implement. Management take these meetings seriously and see the benefit in ensuring that prisoners feel that their grievances are heard.

Wing Representative

Any prisoner can apply to be a 'Wing Representative' and then represent the prisoners on their wing. If the application is approved, the prisoner will be expected to attend Prisoner Consultative Committee meetings (above).

Prisoners who have been selected to represent their wing are expected to be mature people and to be able to put across their views in a coherent and non-aggressive way. They must be willing to engage in debate with prison staff, without losing sight of the fact that they are representing the views of the whole wing.

Taking on this role can be a big responsibility, as it is not easy to please all prisoners at all times. Having a reasonable level of self-confidence is quite helpful, especially when dealing with prison managers.

Toe-by-Toe and Read and Grow (Literacy)

An established system for tackling illiteracy (including through dyslexia) is the Shannon Trust's Toe-by-Toe where mentors from amongst prisoners are trained to encourage and support prisoners with little or no reading skills. They provide informal, one-to-one learning opportunities on the wings and in other parts of the prison. Another good system is Read and Grow, which also uses a one-to-one approach together with a unique 'phonic alphabet' in which each object is shaped like the letter it represents. Prisoners should ask about these and other schemes on their wing.

Violence Reduction Prison Representative (VR Rep)

The prisoner who normally fulfils this role commonly wears a bright orange T-shirt with 'Violence Reduction' emblazoned on the back of it (The colour may vary from prison-to-prison).

The primary role of a VR rep is to provide support to prisoners who have been bullied, victimised or attacked by other prisoners. Anyone who goes to see a 'VR rep' will be given the option of filling out a VR form, which can then be passed on to the VR officer on the wing. An incident can then be officially investigated and action taken by wing staff. A victim could then be moved to another wing or placed on the prison's protection wing, the attacker or bully could be punished by having privileges taken away, or the wing manager may try to bring both prisoners together and attempt to find a way in which any unpleasantness can be avoided in the future.

Diversity Representative

As with VR reps (above), 'Diversity reps' will also wear a coloured T-shirt, this time with the word 'Diversity' written across the back. They, too, provide support to those prisoners who feel that they are being victimised, due to a characteristic that is protected by the Equality Act 2010. Discrimination of any type is not tolerated once the authorities are made aware of it. A diversity rep can ensure that stringent measures are taken to ensure that the discrimination is stopped in its tracks.

The prison system is not exempt from having 'ignorant' people living or working in its midst. As in the real world, there are always people who think it is okay to make life difficult for those who are not like them. Thankfully, the days when prejudice was acceptable are rapidly coming to an end, but there is still much more work to be done to fully combat racial and gender discrimination, and transphobia within our jails, but it is reassuring that many men and women are fully committed to doing just that.

Insiders

These are selected prisoners/trainee volunteers providing basic information and reassurance to other prisoners, especially during the early stages of a sentence.

Classroom Support Mentor

A prisoner who has been approved to be a mentor (after application to the prison's Education Department) may have different roles, depending on which prison they are in. In some, they are a classroom assistant; in others they may accompany a teacher who provides in-cell education to prisoners who are unable to get to the Education Department. Some prisoners are paid for this, while some do it on a purely voluntary basis. Many mentors teach other prisoners basic Mathematics or English, and provide a valuable addition to underfunded education programmes in prisons across Britain.

LIFE IMPRISONMENT

13 Prison Visits

If a prisoner's family is on benefits, they may be able to receive help with the travel costs incurred when visiting the prisoner.

Life-sentenced prisoners are often located in prisons far from their home town. Whether by car or train, travelling is expensive, but the Assisted Prison Visits Unit (APVU) can help with all, or part of the fare, or petrol money. Money can also be provided for food. Many lifers' families do not know that they can receive financial help when visiting their loved ones, and the help provided by the Assisted Prison Visits Scheme Helpline (Tel: 03000 632100) can help prevent families from breaking up.

Many prisons provide lifer/family day visits. These usually take place in the prison visits room. It is an opportunity for the prisoner and his or her family to spend up to seven hours together in an informal setting.

These special visits also allow prisoners to spend quality time with their children. Numerous activities are often put on by the prison staff and childcare workers. Prisoners eligible for these visits may have to be on Enhanced regime (see *Section 1*), and 'adjudication free' (see *Section 28*) for at least six months.

There is always a big demand for these visits, and it is normally a case of first come, first served.

LIFE IMPRISONMENT

14 Open Conditions

The process used by open prisons to progress a life-sentenced prisoner towards release is similar in most open jails. Soon after arrival, the prisoner can expect to be interviewed by their lifer manager, the Probation Service and maybe a psychologist.

They will work together to assess the individual prisoner's needs and decide what support they are going to require. They could decide to return the prisoner to closed conditions, if, say, an offending behaviour course that had once been recommended has, for some reason, not been completed.

If it is felt that the prisoner should remain in open conditions, they can expect to go through a number of stages. The length of time between those stages will depend on many factors, for example, when their next Parole Board hearing is due, whether they are pre-tariff or post-tariff (see *Section 3*), any learning difficulties or disabilities they may have, or whether they have previously failed in open conditions.

A lifer can expect to be given a list of dates by their offender manager, which should provide them with an idea of when they will become eligible to work in the community, have town visits, etc. This is a rough guide:

Stage 1	Arrive in open prison
Stage 2	Start completing supervised voluntary work in the community

Stage 3	Start completing unsupervised work (voluntary or paid)
Stage 4	Start having town visits
Stage 5	Start having resettlement (home) leaves to home address or hostel
Stage 6	(Hopefully) receive recommendation for release from the prison
Stage 7	Sit Parole Board
Stage 8	Release with licence conditions set by the Parole Board

If a prisoner arrives at an open prison having only a short time before their next parole hearing is due, they may be expected to defer the hearing until all the above stages have been completed. Refusal to defer could result in them remaining in prison for an extra year or two. They may have their progress set back at any time, for many different reasons, some of which are out of their control.

- London-based offender managers, due to their heavy workload, are 'notoriously' slow in finalising reports, and they amy find it difficult to attend post-course meetings, sentence planning sessions and parole boards.

- Any perceived increase in risk to the public could lead to a prisoner being grounded (stopped from working outside the prison) or returned to a closed prison.

- A positive test for cannabis may lead to an official warning and adjudication, plus a grounding.

- A positive test for any Class A drug (e.g. heroin or cocaine) will, in 99% of cases, lead to the prisoner being returned immediately to closed conditions.

- Possession of a mobile phone is punished severely in open prisons. Although most inmates will use their phones to call their loved ones, the prison authorities will always see mobile phones as a threat to security and a potential means of intimidating witnesses or committing offences, such as arranging drugs deals.

- If a prisoner complains about anything and the staff feel that they may abscond, they will be returned to closed conditions.

- If a prisoner has his or her parole denied, they could also be returned to a closed prison, if the staff suspect they may abscond.

- If a prisoner on home leave or hostel resettlement leave breaks his or her licence conditions, they could be recalled, or arrested and sent to, a closed prison.

- A prisoner on a town visit (see *Section 6*) or working in the community can also be returned to a closed prison if they have broken their licence conditions. If a prisoner on a town visit wishes to engage in an activity not mentioned in their temporary licence, they should consider: (a) whether the prison would allow it; and (b) whether the prison would be able to justify what the prisoner has done to the Secretary of State as part of the resettlement process.

LIFE IMPRISONMENT

15 Release on Temporary Licence (ROTL)

There are many reasons why a lifer could be released on temporary licence. It is unusual for a ROTL to be granted to any lifer in Category-A, B or C conditions. Any life-sentenced prisoner wanting ROTL will have to be able to demonstrate that they can be trusted to interact with the public, not to commit any offence and to return to prison at the time specified on their licence. Prisoners in some open (Category-D) prisons will be able to receive ROTL for hospital or dental appointments, but most ROTLs tend to be issued to prisoners who have completed the required period of supervised community work and are moving on to unsupervised community work, and/or resettlement hostel leave.

Licence Conditions

Licence conditions are pretty much standard for all lifers. In general, prisoners must:

- obey all conditions in the licence;

- go only where they have permission to go;

- not be in the company of anyone under 18-years-of-age;

- not enter licensed premises (pub, bar or restaurant); and

- not drive a car without permission of the prison.

In most open prisons, whilst on a town visit (see *Section 6*), you can usually go anywhere within a 15-mile radius of the prison, subject to approval.

Before going on an unescorted town visit, you must seek permission from the prison to engage in certain activities with your family or friends. This is because the prison would not allow a prisoner to engage in any activity unless it would clearly be of benefit to their reintegration into society (and not embarrass the prison authorities if the media took an interest in an individual prisoner's resettlement activities!)

16 Lifer Recall

When a lifer is recalled to prison, it is usually because the supervising probation officer feels that he or she presents a risk to the public. The Secretary of State can also recall a lifer on the recommendation of the Parole Board, or acting alone.

The decision will then be looked at by the Parole Board, and the lifer will be entitled to know why he or she has been recalled, to receive copies of all documents that will be presented to the Parole Board, and to make personal written representations.

First and foremost, the board will focus on the risk to the public posed by the prisoner, and whether the actions which invoked the recall can be linked to the lifer's original offence.

Recall powers

The Parole Board has the power to release lifers (including mandatory lifers) immediately, if they consider that the recall was not necessary for the protection of the public. The board may defer their decision, especially if the lifer is facing further charges.

If it is considered that the recall was appropriate, the lifer will then continue serving their sentence in the same way as before their release.

Concerns have been raised about the role of the Parole Board, especially in situations where it has recalled a lifer, and is then expected to decide whether the decision was appropriate.

A Job for a Solicitor

A recalled lifer should employ the services of a solicitor who is familiar with the recall procedure. Various firms of solicitors specialise in prison law (a selection of advertisements can be found, e.g. in the regular prison newspaper *Inside Time*).

This solicitor should contact the Parole Board, asking the reason for the recall, when the board will be sitting to decide whether the lifer should be re-released, or, alternatively, how the lifer should address the behaviour which contributed towards the recall, before the next Parole Board sits.

17 Driving Lessons

If a lifer wishes to take driving lessons, it may be possible to do so, once they are in an open prison. First of all, they would need to send in an application form for a provisional licence, with their birth certificate and two passport-sized photos.

The form and the photos could be obtained on an escorted town visit (*Section 3*). Once the provisional licence has arrived, they would need to find the address of the nearest theory test centre, then apply for release on temporary licence ROTL (*Section 15*) or an escorted town visit to complete the test.

More applications for ROTL would be necessary in order to take the lessons with an approved instructor and the final driving-test with an examiner.

18 Travelling Abroad After Release

A lifer, once released on licence, could, one day, be allowed to travel abroad for work or holiday. They would first have to seek permission from their probation officer, and they would be unlikely to obtain this permission until they had spent a few years in the community.

Even if permission is granted, a lifer on licence can normally only expect only to be allowed to travel to countries within the European Union.

A lifer who wishes to move abroad permanently must have an unblemished record for at least ten years following release on licence and must successfully apply to have the life licence terminated.

It is important that the lifer discusses his or her plans with their probation officer. Failure to do so could result in a recall to prison, as the probation officer may feel that the lifer is not being transparent.

Lifers who are not British citizens must also seek permission before travelling abroad.

19 Personality Disorder

Many lifers and inmates serving indeterminate sentences for public protection (IPP) (where these are still in effect) may have been diagnosed as having a personality disorder of a psychopathic-type.[4] Broadly speaking, this means that prisoners in this category have limited empathy, which allows them to create victims because they are unable to comprehend how a victim feels.

One school of thought is that these prisoners are untreatable, untrustworthy, and compulsive liars. They may often possess superficial charm, and are ruthless and manipulative.

However, there is another view — that they can be treated, if they engage in cognitive behaviour therapy (CBT).

Interviews with a Psychologist

Dangerous and severe personality disorder (DSPD) Units were set up to contain such prisoners, and it is likely that they will remain there for many years. Some may be held in a secure hospital (formerly known as a 'special hospital') such as Broadmoor or Rampton: see also *Section 25*.

During a lifer's sentence, it is usual for him or her to be interviewed before every Parole Board hearing by a psychologist, who will be expected to provide a report assessing the prisoner's risk to the public. As well as psychometric tests,

---

[4] For a basic guide to a complex topic, including how the PCL-R works, see *Psychopaths: An Introduction* by Herschel Prins, published in 2013 by Waterside Press.

prisoners will usually complete a Hare Pyschopathy Checklist-Revised (PCL-R).

These instruments help the psychologist to predict the likelihood of a prisoner reoffending in the future. If a prisoner scores highly on the PCL-R, the Parole Board will expect him or her to have completed offending behaviour courses, before recommending that they be transferred to a less secure prison.

A prisoner's risk to the public is paramount in the mind of report writers and the Parole Board.

There are, however, many lifers with borderline or high PCL-R scores who nay find it very hard to achieve release. Although often highly intelligent people who score highly in 'Raven' IQ tests, they may also have a tendency to manipulate those around them, and although able to convince some people of their remorse, find it difficult to convince some members of the Parole Board, psychologists and supervisors.

Deception may come naturally to them. Possibly, what makes them particularly dangerous is their inability to see their own faults or take responsibility for their actions. In their eyes, any misfortune that befalls them is always someone else's fault. They may see themselves as superior and struggle in situations and social groups where their views are challenged.

To make their personality 'cocktail' yet more dangerous, they may also tend towards impulsivity and lack of insight into the consequences of their actions. Generally, when hurting, they hurt others, sometimes with terrible, even fatal results.

But not all psychopaths are dangerous. They can be everywhere. Some are politicians, leaders of industry, professionals, sportspeople or entertainers and may pass unnoticed unless they do something criminal; others may be *you* or *me*!!

20 Prison Politics

There is a saying that if you want to remain friends you should never discuss religion or politics. To avoid conflict situations in jail, you should stay away from gossip, rumour and speculation.

There are prisoners who will try to manipulate you into attacking other prisoners, or to act in a way that would get you into trouble. Prisoners will do this for entertainment, and 'a laugh' as you get dragged down to the segregation unit.

When someone tries to tell you about someone else's crime, or says that someone is a 'grass', it's best to say that you are not interested in other people's problems and that you have enough problems of your own. You came to prison on your own and will be leaving on your own.

Ultimately, you have to trust your own judgement in deciding whom to trust in prison. Don't try to impress others and don't be impressed by others. Your goal must always be to get out of prison as soon as possible and get on with your life.

Beware Those Prisoners Who Will Bring You Down!
There are always prisoners in jail who don't care whether they get out or not, and they definitely don't care about *your* future. The more you try to turn your life around, the more they will try to drag you back where they are!

It can be easy, especially for lifers, to forget about the outside world. To think about the reasons which brought you to prison can be painful, and easier to block out. For some, this pain is so bad that they only feel better by making other prisoners' lives a nightmare.

Don't get involved in things that do not concern you, keep yourself to yourself as best you can, don't spread rumours, don't get involved in others' arguments, think of the possible consequences of the things you say and do, but most of all, *be safe*!

21 Bullying

Prison can bring out the best and the worst qualities in prisoners. If a person has antisocial qualities or holds antisocial beliefs in the community, it is more than likely that he or she will demonstrate these same qualities and beliefs within the prison environment.

There are others, however, who are quite passive and unassuming outside, but in prison may try to dominate, intimidate and exploit weaker colleagues in an attempt to make themselves feel more powerful. It is a common occurrence for prisoners who lack self-confidence and self-esteem to become bullies, as they try to assert themselves and control others in an attempt to increase their own status.

Some do this by selling tobacco, then charging extortionate rates of interest. Others sell drugs. Some, in shared cells, act in an aggressive manner by imposing their choice of TV programmes, also controlling what goes on in the cell.

There are prisoners who make fun of those who are different or less well-off.

In some prisons, inmates have been bullied because they do not have the 'right' trainers, are homosexual, lesbian or trans-sexual, or are perhaps better-educated than the majority of the prisoners they live with. It does not help if you stick out in prison.

Unfortunately, the result is that many leave prison with an even worse attitude than they came in with, feel even less empathy towards others, and soon return to prison.

In my view, evil definitely prevails. 'It only takes,' as Edmund Burke said, 'good men do nothing'. It should be applauded that prisons now acknowledge bullying as the serious problem that it is and there are anti-bullying schemes in most prisons about which you should enquire if you are on the receiving end.

Violence Reduction and Standing Up to Bullies

Violence reduction prisoner representatives are now being appointed to help combat bullying and violence in our jails. They provide support to those who are being bullied, and should be the first point of contact if a prisoner wants to make an official complaint about their abuser.

It takes a brave person to stand up to bullies in prison, as anyone who does so risks ridicule and further bullying by others. However, it is hoped that in the future bullying will be reduced by showing that this behaviour will not be tolerated in any form, and will be punished by loss of privileges and/or adjudication.

22 Same Sex Relationships

This is clearly an issue that is still considered taboo, especially within male prisons. Sexual relationships in prison are illegal, as a prison is technically classed as a public place, and any sexual activity is deemed as being occurring in public. Male prisoners engaging in such activity can, in theory, be charged with committing an act of gross indecency.

All prisoners should remember that there is a life for them outside prison, and that they would not wish, once released, to pass on any diseases or infections they may have caught whilst in prison. It is possible that some prisoners may lie to potential sexual partners about their sexual health, or not inform them about any problem they may have. In these circumstances, intercourse should be avoided, as the possible consequences can be life threatening. It should be noted that someone could be a carrier of the AIDS or hepatitis virus, without showing any outward signs of illness.

Ideally, condoms would be provided to male prisoners. However, once staff become aware of such a request, separation of the parties concerned is likely, in the interest of good order and discipline. But enforced separation can result in the same emotional trauma as the loss of a loved one in any other circumstances. Furthermore, there is the risk of being subjected to ridicule and persecution from other inmates.

Beware Emotional Pitfalls

Prisoners should therefore be aware of the emotional pitfalls of forming close relationships within prisons. When individuals are thrown together in a claustrophobic environment, maybe in a shared cell, sometimes for many years, it is not unknown for sexual relationships to develop (rather than just not be spoken of).

Sexual activity amongst male prisoners is still generally viewed as deviant behaviour by both staff and prisoners alike. Unfortunately and despite laws against sexual discrimination and hate crime, there is nowhere within the prison system (except, possibly, a Listener, *Sections 1* and *12* of this book, or maybe the chaplain of their own particular faith) for prisoners to turn to for help or advice about sexual feelings they may be experiencing.

23 Drugs and Healthcare

Drug use is something that lifers and IPP sentenced prisoners in particular have to guard against. Serving an indeterminate sentence, with no release date, is extremely difficult, and it is so easy to be tempted to use drugs, especially at times when you may feel lonely, scared or vulnerable.

Drugs may seem to be the best solution—but they will only help in the short-term. The odds are that you will be caught with them eventually, and you will have damaged your chances of release, sometimes close to your tariff date.

Many prisoners come into prison after spending a lifetime in the community using illegal and prescribed drugs. They will *not* get away with using drugs and the consequences for indeterminate-sentenced prisoners are *always* severe. When preparing progress reports or parole reports, drug users will always be recommended to complete further courses to address their drug use, setting back their chances of progression, possibly for a very long time indeed.

Drug-testing

In prison, drug-testing can be mandatory (i.e. enforced whatever the prisoner's wishes) or voluntary. These are known as mandatory drug-testing (MDT) and voluntary drug-testing (VDT), respectively. In some prisons and cell-space permitting it is possible to ask to be placed on a 'drug-free wing'.

Some people believe that many prisoners switched from

using cannabis to heroin because heroin leaves the body more quickly and is unlikely to make a prisoner fail drug tests. It is true that heroin can be undetectable after 48 hours. On an indeterminate sentence, you will be watched and your behaviour monitored more closely than if you were serving a fixed term. Refusal to give drug test samples when required will also set back your progress through the prison system.

CARATS

The CARATS team, which exists in most prisons, is there to help prisoners conquer their drug habit. They are not there to punish or inform on people. The service is confidential and it is in the prisoner's best interests to be as open and honest as possible. CARAT stands for 'counselling, assessment, referral advice, throughcare'.

Smackheads

In the mid-to-late-1980s, especially after the years of publicity which linked them to AIDS, heroin users in prison used this drug in secret. Even those closest to them would not have known. When heroin users *were* discovered, they would often be attacked or have their cells 'burnt out', as prisoners generally believed that all 'smackheads' were potential cell thieves and AIDS sufferers.

From the early-1990s, when people became more educated about the perils of heroin misuse (and before regular drug-testing was introduced into British prisons), there was an increase in all types of drug use. This increase in the use of illegal drugs may have been mirrored outside of prison. Rightly or wrongly, the 'rave' scene of the 1980s has been held responsible for the early promotion of the drugs Ecstasy or MDMA. When users of these drugs came to prison, they brought in with them a less defined idea of which drugs were morally good or bad. Heroin use soon became a less shameful activity amongst prisoners, when they realised that it was not true that all people who use heroin rob old ladies of their handbags, or spread AIDS.

Drugs and Lifers

No sane person would condone the use of drugs in prison. They can lead to chaos in a prisoner's life. Debt, depression, emotional instability, addiction and family or relationship breakdowns may all have their roots in illicit drug use. It would be almost impossible to convince a prisoner with a personality disorder that it is in their best interest to stop taking drugs. They would like to think that they can always control their own drug use, and that a drug's ability to create an addict is no match for the willpower of a psychopath!

So, when a prisoner receives a life-sentence and could potentially spend the rest of his or her life behind bars, how can he or she realistically be expected to live without drugs? Until the 1990s, lifers could go to the prison doctor and relatively easily be prescribed drugs such as Valium and DF118s. It was acknowledged that to separate people from society for life was not normal, and that medication could be a useful tool in preventing odd, bizarre and unmanageable behaviour which the sentence in itself could cause. Even though some of these prisoners have committed inhumane acts on victims, maybe a balance needs to be found to ensure that not only do victims and their families feel they have received justice for the hurt done to them, but that hope is also within the reach of all those in prison so that they do not desire drugs.

Prescription Drugs

The maxim used by some prison staff is that they should 'believe nothing and question everything'. Obtaining a prescription for painkillers can be difficult, as the more cynical healthcare staff and doctors believe that prisoners just want to abuse drugs. Generalising in this way can lead to a prisoner (who really should be treated as a patient in this regard) being left in pain. Prisoners experiencing healthcare difficulties should contact their solicitor.

24 Money Management

Although it is possible for lifers to accumulate significant amounts of money in their spending and private cash accounts, it is impossible for a prisoner to open a bank or building society account in person from within prison. Only whilst on a town visit (*Section 3*) from an open prison is it possible to do this oneself. By applying to the prisoners' money clerk, it is possible to have money transferred into a prison savings account, but the money will receive no interest.

By using a cash disbursement form, a prisoner can send money to a friend or partner, who may open an account in their name. Prisoners who already have money in an account but do not have their bank details, passbook or card should write to the bank's head office and ask for their advice. There is also a possibility that the interest on the savings of a serving prisoner may be exempt from tax. A letter to the bank or building society's manager should be the prisoner's first step in finding out if this would apply in his or her case.

Saving for the Future

Once a lifer has spent a period of time in an open prison, he may become eligible for paid work in the community. If he or she does not have a bank account, a prison officer may be available to escort him to a bank and provide the identification necessary to open an account.

The Lifer Unit or Community Placement Team may ask

to see bank books or statements from any prisoner on paid work. They will want to know how the prisoner is managing his or her money, that it is not, e.g. coming from some illicit source, and whether or not he or she is saving for the future.

A lifer will always be held to account for any of his or her actions, regardless of what they may be. Refusal to give prison staff or an offender manager banking details could result in the prisoner being returned to closed conditions.

Any prisoner having trouble managing his money should seek advice from his lifer manager, who may suggest attending Money Management Classes.

25 Mental Health Issues

Unfortunately, there are many mentally-ill prisoners. It would appear that if you have been diagnosed as suffering from a mental illness for which 'an appropriate medical treatment is available', such as schizophrenia, you may spend some time in prison before being allocated to a secure hospital, like Rampton or Broadmoor.

Prison Hospital Transfers and Remissions
Ideally, your release would be decided by a medical health tribunal. Sadly there are many prisoners who, sent or transferred to a secure hospital, have been returned to the prison system (sometimes called 'remission'), where they face extreme difficulty in achieving release. There are also instances of prisoners being sent to secure hospitals for assessment, staying there for years, then being sent back to prison to continue serving their sentence, yet the time spent in the secure hospital has not been counted as part of the time they have served in custody.

Mental Illness Amongst Prisoners: Quite a Problem
It is estimated that over 30 per cent of prisoners, including lifers and IPP prisoners, have mental health issues. Many of these receive adequate support and treatment to help them progress through the prison system. This is not a new problem, yet it is one that the justice system is struggling to address.

Engaging with the Healthcare Team

Prisoners with mental health issues need to work closely with the healthcare team within their prison, to ensure that their needs are met. By engaging with the healthcare team, these prisoners stand the best chance of receiving the support that is needed for their condition.

26 Self-Harm

Many prisoners self-harm, in many different ways and for many different reasons, but the fact that someone is serving a life-sentence can be part of this. Some self-harm in secret, but many injure themselves so seriously that they require medical assistance. It is important that you speak to someone as soon as you start feeling that you want to harm yourself. Psychotherapy is not easily accessible in prisons, but there are other people who are willing to provide support.

Listeners (*Section 12*) are available in most prisons. They are prisoners who have been trained by the Samaritans. Whatever you tell them is in the strictest confidence. The only exceptions to this are if you mean to kill yourself or harm others. Listeners breaching this code of confidentiality will be expelled from the Samaritans.

In-reach teams are easy to contact within prison and can provide mental health specialists who can treat you or provide specialist support.

Depression and Other Causes
If you feel that you are depressed or something else is driving you to self-harm, there is no shame in speaking to the prison doctor. He can refer you to a psychiatrist who can prescribe medication to help you. Prison doctors and healthcare workers are no strangers to the issues surrounding self-harmers.

Other Kinds of Support

It is easy to feel that you are serving your sentence alone and that no-one cares if you live or die. There are many people who are willing to help. However, the first step must be made by you.

The prison library can give you the telephone number for the Samaritans, and some prisons even provide a phone connected directly to their helpline. Ask your wing staff or Listener scheme if this service is available. Members of the chaplaincy can also be approached via chapel or application. They can put you in touch with a support network and give you good, trustworthy advice.

27 Hygiene

As unpleasant as this subject is, it is one that prisoners need to be aware of. The personal hygiene of many individuals, both inside and outside of prison, leaves a lot to be desired. The risk of becoming infected is greater when you live in an enclosed environment where airborne viruses can spread like wildfire.

Fungal infections are also easily spread, as prisoners are not provided with flip-flops to wear in showers, and only some inmates choose to buy them.

Avoiding Infection
The inability of many prisoners to wash their hands after going to the toilet is a problem in prisons, where the prisoner then touches door handles and railings, risking infecting a whole wing with streptococcus or E coli. The risk of infection can be even worse for cell-mates who share cigarettes, use games console controllers and cutlery together with those who have no interest in their own personal hygiene.

If you are concerned about the risks of catching hepatitis in prison, an application to the healthcare centre is the first step towards protecting yourself with the hepatitis jab. Wash your hands and be careful what you touch!

28 Adjudications

Breaches of the Prison Rules may result in a charge being brought against the prisoner and what is known as an 'adjudication'. Often, cases will be heard in the prison's segregation unit and in front of either a visiting district judge or a prison governor depending on whether the matter is a routine infringement or a more serious matter involving days being added to a sentence.

Governors may deal with prisoners under the Incentives and Earned Privileges Scheme (see *Section 1*) usually leading to a reduction in their privilege level and a negative entry in their wing record. Adjudicating governors are expected to be unbiased, but, in my experience, tend to believe prison officers giving evidence, which is one reason why judges were introduced after challenges in the European Court of Human Rights. Even so, many prisoners choose to admit guilt, even when they are innocent, in order to receive a lesser penalty than they would be given if found guilty!

In more serious cases, the visiting judge will hear the evidence, listen to the prisoner's defence, take account of whether he or she has pleaded guilty or not guilty, and consider any mitigating circumstances. He or she will then decide whether the prisoner guilty and if so pass sentence.

There are a wide range of sentences and orders, again depending on the respective powers of the judge or governor. These include a suspended sentence, a fine, restrictions on the use of private cash, stoppage of earnings, a combination of some of these, a period of time in the segregation unit, also known as cellular confinement (CC), or 'extra days', i.e. days added to the prisoners original sentence.

Segregation

Segregation means that prisoner will spend a number of days isolated from the rest of the prison in the Segregation Block (or 'Seg'), deprived of all privileges—no TV, in-cell electricity, or hi-fi, etc. Prisoners can expect to see a governor, doctor and a member of the Independent Monitoring Board (IMB) every day they are segregated. The purpose of this is to ensure that the prisoner is healthy, not being mistreated and able to voice any concerns they may have about their treatment.

Each prisoner is entitled to 30 minutes' exercise per day and to receive their canteen (prison shop) goods, unless their punishment forbids it.

Prisoners who are aggressive towards segregation officers can expect to be placed in a strip cell, minus their clothing, with a canvas top and shorts to wear (to prevent suicide) and one strip cell blanket.

Reassessment of Privileges

Although seen as unfair, a prisoner adjudicated against and punished can also expect to have their privilege level (*Section 1*) reassessed, once they have returned to their wing.

Calling in the Police

If the matter in question amounts to a crime, particularly a serious one, this may be passed to the police to investigate.

29 Artificial Insemination

For couples wishing to have a child whilst one partner is in prison serving a life-sentence (and hence with the prospect that a child could not be conceived otherwise), conception may be possible via artificial insemination. The couple would have to apply to the Secretary of State, who has told the Grand Chamber of the European Court of Human Rights that each case will be judged on its individual merits, taking into account Convention principles.

The British Government produced statistics to the Grand Chamber demonstrating that the individual assessment was genuine. By 2011, 28 applications for artificial insemination facilities had been made since 1996. Twelve were not pursued, one was withdrawn, one applicant was released on parole, and two were pending. Of the remaining 12 applications, three were granted and nine refused.

Challenges in the European Court

A number of applicants who were refused access to artificial insemination facilities challenged the Secretary of State via the European Court. The government emphasised that a policy of restricting access was 'a necessary consequence of imprisonment' and that 'public confidence in the prison system would be undermined if the punitive and deterrent elements of a sentence could be circumvented by allowing prisoners guilty of certain serious offences to conceive children'.

According to the Secretary of State, the government's policy is as follows.

Requests by prisoners for artificial insemination are carefully considered on individual merit and will only be granted in exceptional circumstances. In reaching decisions, particular attention is given to the following general considerations:

1. Whether the provision of artificial insemination facilities is the only means by which conception is likely to occur.

2. Whether the prisoner's expected day of release is neither so near that delay would not be excessive, nor so distant that he/she would be unable to assume the responsibilities of a parent.

3. Whether both parties want the procedure and the medical authorities both inside and outside the prison are satisfied that the couple are medically fit to proceed with artificial insemination.

4. Whether the couple were in a well-established and stable relationship prior to imprisonment, which is likely to subsist after the prisoner's release.

5. Whether there is any evidence to suggest that the couple's domestic circumstances and the arrangements for the welfare of the child are satisfactory, including the time for which the child may expect to be without a father or a mother.

6. Whether, having regard to the prisoner's history, antecedents and other relevant factors, there is evidence to suggest that it

would not be in the public interest to provide artificial insemination facilities in a particular case.

If you and your partner wish to have access to these facilities, contact your solicitor and ask him to make an application to the Secretary of State.

The Grand Chamber also established that more than half of the contracting States allow for conjugal visits for prisoners (subject to a variety of restrictions). However, while the court has expressed its approval for the evolution in several European countries towards conjugal visits, it has not yet interpreted the Convention as requiring contracting States to make provision for such visits. It appears, at this time, that it will be many more years before the British government allows prisoners access to conjugal visits.

LIFE IMPRISONMENT

30 Complaints Procedures

The Internal HMPS Complaints System

If you wish to make an official complaint about the way you have been treated in prison, it is important to follow the complaints procedure, which can be summarised as follows:

Step 1   Fill in an official prison complaints form as fully as possible.

Step 2   Ensure that it is logged by wing staff in their complaints/applications book.

Step 3   Wait for the answer, which normally takes around two weeks.

- If your complaint is about a member of staff, the Governor could ask the police to investigate the matter.
- You may ask for an envelope to put your 'Request and Complaints Form' (R&C Form) in. this is called a 'Confidential access envelope'.

Step 4   If you are dissatisfied with the answer, you can ask for an appeal form and submit it to the Prison Service Area Manager, who will also look into your complaint. This appeal can also be sent in a confidential access envelope and the reply may take several weeks.

Independent Monitoring Board (IMB)

You can also or instead make a written request to speak to a member of the Independent Monitoring Board (IMB). Board members are independent of HMPS and staff and ultimately report to the Justice Secretary. There should be IMB forms on your wing and a 'yellow box' in which to place them. The IMB is made up of members of the public, some of whom may be magistrates (also called justices of the peace (JPs)).

Prisons and Probation Ombudsman

The Prisons and Probation Ombudsman can also help if a prisoner is not satisfied, after going through the internal complaints procedure. A prisoner must write to the ombudsman within one month of receiving the final internal response to their complaint. It is important that the prisoner encloses copies of all paperwork regarding their complaint, to include the request and complaints form and the appeal, together with the responses, as well as any Independent Monitoring Board (IMB) responses. The address of the Ombudsman is given at the end of the book.

Members of Parliament

A prisoner needing help or advice can also write to the Member of Parliament for the constituency in which the prison is located. They could also write to the MP whose constituency includes their home address. Alternatively, the prisoner's family could write to their MP on the prisoner's behalf.

Race and Other Discrimination

If a prisoner feels he or she is being discriminated against because of their race, complaints forms should be available on his wing ('Racist Incident Reporting Form'), as well as a box to put them in. They may also report the incident to the prison's race relations liaison officer (RRLO), who is attached to the Race Relations Management Team that exists in every prison. On their wing, there may also be a diversity representative who can help with a complaint. Discrimination against a person's race, colour, religion or gender is taken very seriously by HM Prison Service and will not be tolerated.

LIFE IMPRISONMENT

31 Access to Official Files

If a lifer wishes to see any of the files held on him or her, there are a number of ways that he or she can seek to do this.

- To see their medical file, or have it copied, a request needs to be made to the healthcare manager. A charge may be made to the prisoner for any copies requested. The cost is usually something like ten pence per page.

- To see the wing file, a request would need to be made to the wing manager.

- To see information held by the psychology department or Probation Service, a solicitor would be needed to submit an official request.

- I obtained my official files fromt
  The Information Manager
  Building 16
  S & T Store
  Burton Road
  Branston
  Burton-upon-Trent
  Staffordshire
  DE14 3EG

Under the Data Protection Act, prisoners are entitled to see all data that is held on them (although some information may be withheld to protect third parties, or to prevent or detect crime). The prisoner will have to send a payment of £10 via a cash disbursement form. It may take a month or two, to receive all the data that the Prison Service holds.

32 The Criminal Injuries Compensation Authority (CICA)

If a prisoner is attacked at any time, they may be eligible to receive a payment from CICA. The injury must be directly attributable to a crime of violence, including arson or poisoning. But there are many reasons why an award may be withheld.

1. If the prisoner fails to co-operate with the police or other authority in attempting to bring the assailant to justice.

2. If the prisoner fails to give all reasonable assistance to the authority, other body or person in connection with the attack.

3. If the conduct of the victim before, during or after the incident makes it inappropriate that a full award should be made, or any award at all.

4. If the prisoner's character, as shown by their criminal convictions (excluding convictions spent under the Rehabilitation of Offenders Act 1974 at the date of the application or death) or by evidence available to the claims officer makes it inappropriate that a full award be made, or any award at all.

The claims officer may also withhold or reduce an award where it is considered that excessive consumption of alcohol or use of illicit drugs by the claimant contributed to the circumstances which gave rise to the injury, in such a way as to make it inappropriate that a full, or any, award be made at all. The CICA will take into account the prisoner's criminal record and give a score for each unspent conviction. If a prisoner scores ten penalty points or more, he will usually receive nothing. If the decision is made to give no award, the prisoner can appeal, but this is unlikely to make any difference, especially if he has an extensive criminal history.

Information on how to apply for an award is available by writing to CICA: see the address at the end of this book.

The CICA is also unlikely to make an award if the prisoner is seeking compensation by other means.

Decisions made by the CICA may not be challenged by way of judicial review, and the authority will always take into account how their decision might be perceived by the general public.

In 2012, it was announced that the threshold below which payments would be made would be raised, thus excluding a greater number of small claims.

33 Criminal Cases Review Commission (CCRC)

If a prisoner has appealed his or her conviction and not been happy with the result, or if he or she believes they have been the victim of a miscarriage of justice, they could write to:

Criminal Cases Review Commission
Alpha Tower
Suffolk Street
Queensway
Birmingham
B1 1TT

The CCRC will send an application form on which the prisoner should include as much information as possible.

The time that it takes to review the case will depend on its complexity. The CCRC will only be able to help if there is a new argument or evidence that was not available at the time of the trial or appeal.

If it is felt that the case should not be referred to the Court of Appeal, the prisoner could still submit an application for leave to appeal out of time. If the application for leave to appeal, or an appeal, is unsuccessful, it is possible to make a further appeal to the CCRC.

LIFE IMPRISONMENT

34 The High Court, Court of Appeal, Supreme Court and European Court of Human Rights

The Actions of Government

In a democratic country the law is there to prevent abuse of power and authority. So, never be put off from challenging the administrative actions of, say, the Ministry of Justice (or other Government department or public bodies where appropriate), even in the final resort taking them to the High Court. You might get legal aid to do this (although this is currently under scrutiny), and your solicitor should be familiar with the processes, including those for judicial review., i.e. review by a senior judge of administrative action.

However, do be warned that it can be a long and sometimes fruitless process so it is always worth looking for another, ready solution first. It is also important to remember that the High Court cannot force Government to do anything except reconsider the action or decision that you are challenging; although it will often comply with court rulings.

If the High Court rules in your favour, and, e.g. the ministry challenges the court's recommendations, you may have to take your appeal through the higher courts, and finally to the Supreme Court, now the highest court in England and Wales, which in 2009 replaced the House of Lords.

The European Court

Whether in respect of court decisions or administrative action, before taking your case to the European Court of Human Rights, it is expected that you will have first used the British legal system, and be appealing to the European Court as a last resort. Doing this may take some years, and there is no guarantee that the British courts, the Government or the Ministry will accept or act upon a ruling from the European Court. However, there is a long tradition of serving prisoners challenging the UK Government in Europe leading to positive outcomes and changes to the system on occasions.

Appeals Against Conviction or Sentence

If you are appealing against your non-mandatory sentence[5] or underlying conviction, you should note, to avoid disappointment, that though the Court of Appeal may hear your case, it will not necessarily rule in your favour. In most cases of appeal against conviction, it will not even hear the appeal unless there is new evidence that was not made available at your trial.

If you wish to appeal the length or variety of your sentence or conviction, it is important to get your solicitor to progress this as soon as possible, otherwise you will have to apply to appeal 'out of time'. He or she will normally appoint a barrister to look at the case and decide whether it merits going to appeal.

All prisoners have the right to apply for an appeal, or at least obtain legal advice, so that you can weigh up their chances of success. If your solicitor advises against appealing, you may

---

[5] There is no appeal against a mandatory life-sentence as such, although there may be against the tariff which is set: again seek good legal advice.

wish to choose another who is more supportive or prepared to offer a different opinion (although you may be unlikely to get legal aid twice). If you believe you have been wronged, never give up your challenge.

LIFE IMPRISONMENT

35 Offending Behaviour Courses

At the end of this section, I have added a note of the courses I have completed over the years, to give some idea of those available (although some of them may have been criticised or modified) and the kind of courses that could be added to a prisoner's sentence plan or recommended by the Parole Board.

There have been many cases where short-tariff lifers, lifers who are 'over tariff' or other indeterminate sentence prisoners have been prioritised for offending behaviour courses; equally there are other instances where particular courses are simply not available even though release may depend on completing one of these first. Sometimes it is necessary to request a transfer to another prison where a course is running. Getting the right courses 'under your belt' or 'on your CV' is all part and parcel of serving a life-sentence.

There are still prisoners in the system serving indeterminate sentences for public protection (IPPs) as well as mandatory or discretionary lifers, and those who when they were under-18 received detention during her Majesty's pleasure.

At one point there were over 6,000 prisoners serving an IPP sentence who had been unable to have their sentences commuted to a determinate sentence. Until this happens, or they are released, they, too, will continue to be 'scrabbling' for places such courses. The number of IPP prisoners could in fact increase, as although the IPP sentence was abolished in 2012, it can still be given for offences committed before the date of abolition.

Some IPP tariffs have been as short as 12 months, but the offending behaviour courses that have been put in their sentence plan would take over five years to complete! This is an issue for a prisoner's solicitor to challenge, but it is possible that if the prisoner is considered to present a high or medium risk to the public, then the Parole Board may demand that all the recommended courses are completed.

Strange as it seems, in some cases, a course recommended may not even exist. In other cases, the Parole Board has recommended one-to-one counselling, yet some prisons have been unable to provide this service for lifers. If a prisoner is unable to fulfil a requirement in his or her sentence plan and cannot have it removed, it may be useful to complete another course as an alternative. As always, a solicitor's advice should be sought, especially one who specialises in dealing with lifer Parole Boards.

There are some prisoners, especially among those diagnosed as having a personality disorder of a psychopathic type, on whom offending behaviour courses may have little impact. Some people are, and will remain, resistant to change. It has been said that some personality disordered prisoners are impulsive, unable to learn from past experiences, do not consider the consequences of their actions and repeat behaviour patterns without regard for the impact on other people. Indeed, it has been suggested that personality disordered prisoners may learn skills on courses that will aid them to commit crimes in the future, and be more successful in evading capture.

A Note on Risk
Hopefully, all prisoners will one day be able to get the help they need to lead a more productive life than one where they are being warehoused for years on end. .At present, the Parole Board appears to believe that completing courses and being able to demonstrate positive change are important components in lowering risk. This is unlikely to change whilst there are few alternatives (e.g. Dangerous and Severe Personality Disorder units; or more therapeutic communities).

A main way in which a prisoner's level of risk to the public is measured is by way of the offending behaviour courses they have successfully completed and how they responded to them. This is unlikely to change (regardless of available statistics which demonstrate the ineffectuality of some of these courses).

Some Final Thoughts
Approached with an open-mind, motivation and a desire to change, it is possible to gain insight into why we do what we shouldn't do and learn ways to help us do what we should!

Advice should be sought before applying for any course. If a course *has to be* completed to meet a sentence plan requirement, it is in the prisoner's best interest to be open to the possibility of personal change. In this way, and with willingness, rather than scepticism, information imparted on the courses can be better retained and made use of.

Taking notes during courses can also be helpful to some, as well as completing homework as soon as possible, rather than leaving it to the last minute. However, if someone does not want to sort their head out, no course in the world, no amount of money and no amount of punishment will change them!

I have set out below the courses which I have completed.

Offending Behaviour Courses Completed by the Author

HM Prison Frankland	Anger Management
HM Prison Whitemoor	Anger Management Violent Offender Treatment Programme (VOTP)
HM Prison Swaleside	Lifer Victim Awareness Reasoning and Rehabilitation (R and R)
HM Prison Shepton Mallet	Conflict Management
HM Prison Elmley	Enhanced Thinking Skills (ETS) Prisoners Addressing Substance Related Offending (PASRO) Controlling Anger and Learning to Manage it (CALM)

36 Possessions and Volumetric Control

The amount of personal property that a prisoner is allowed in his or her cell varies from prison to prison. The policy in most prisons is that all property held by the prisoner for personal use should fit into two volumetric control boxes. These blue boxes may be brought to a prisoner's cell periodically by prison staff to check that the property allowance has not been exceeded.

Cooking utensils, food and education materials must also fit into these boxes.

One large item, e.g. a rug, bird and cage (where permitted), or stereo is allowed, and is not measured against the individual prisoner's volumetric control allowance.

Other items exempt from volumetric control are:

- religious and devotional objects
- bedding
- posters on cell picture board
- legal papers.

Excess possessions, i.e. those over and above any fixed or discretionary allowances, are normally held at HM Prison Service stores in Branston, Staffordshire, pending release.

LIFE IMPRISONMENT

37 Tough on Crime, Tough on the Causes of Crime?

Before coming to the end of this book, I would like to say a little more about crime and punishment. It is easy to criticise the methods by which justice is meted-out and implemented in Britain. What is less easy is making proposals for funding and setting up projects that can deliver a holistic means of cutting the recidivism rate.

It might help if the existing Probation Service focused more on an offender's strengths, rather than on his or her weaknesses. In this spirit of encouragement, an offender might be more forthcoming about his or her needs, especially if there were less emphasis on management for management's sake. The Probation Service has a difficult job to do in managing some extremely 'unmanageable people'. They do provide schemes, programmes and projects for offenders, but in many cases the released offender is given little choice but to complete them or risk recall to prison, rather than being 'encouraged'.

Another barrier which may prevent an offender from fully engaging in offender courses run by the Probation Service, and by prisons, is that of class. It has been said that we live in a class-free society, but some would argue that this is not true at all. A young man, raised by a single mother, living on benefits on a slum estate, educated in an underfunded school, with 40 children to a class and no positive role models, is clearly in a different socio-economic class from one raised by well-educated, home-owning parents, who is sent to a fee-paying school where small class numbers and inspiring teachers encourage him to go on to university and lead a more fulfilling life than those for whom prison is an occupational hazard!

No child should be denied the chance to be all they can be. All prisoners were once children, and if they had had more opportunities to build up their confidence, self-esteem and sense of social responsibility, maybe they would not be rotting in prison cells.

If more projects could be put together by people from the same backgrounds and socio-economic class as the offenders, I believe that they would have more success in reducing reoffending than the university graduates who appear to have a monopoly in creating and running these projects at present.

38 Bereavement

It would be fair to say that one of the most difficult things that a prisoner will experience is the death of a loved one. In theory, this news will have been passed on to the prisoner by a prison chaplain, Imam or other religious leader. In practice, this may not always be so.

Apart from the death itself, just as traumatic could be the realisation that the chance is now gone to resolve a difference, an argument, or just to tell the deceased that the prisoner loved them, or forgave them. Or maybe the prisoner needed to be forgiven, it all depends on the situation.

A prisoner may be able to obtain bereavement counselling by submitting an application to the prison chapel. A member of the chaplaincy will sort out any paperwork or application for the prisoner to attend the funeral where this is allowed. HM Prison Service is only required to let a prisoner out of prison to attend a funeral if the deceased was the prisoner's mother, father, wife or child. Grandparents are not a priority, unless there is a way to show that they acted as parents. As with all matters, in prison, the last word lies with the Governor, who has the power to judge each case on its own individual merits. Of course, at a time like this, the prisoner's personal officer should be asked for advice.

Unless the prisoner is going to a funeral from an open prison, it is almost guaranteed that they will be handcuffed to at least one prison officer. The prison governor also has the power to refuse an application to attend, if there is a security concern, such as a risk of absconding or escape.

Most members of staff will be kind and sensitive to a prisoner's feelings at such a time, as they, too, may have experienced the same emotions when they have lost a loved one.

39 Emotional Trauma and Mental Health

Quite apart from bereavement, feelings of deep loss may also be felt by prisoners who are, e.g. going through a divorce or are deprived of contact with their children.

It is not unusual for some prisoners to cut all ties with the outside world, maybe because of shame or embarrassment, or they may struggle with feelings that they have let their friends and family down.

People can feel a deep sense of loneliness both inside and outside of prison. Unfortunately, it is sometimes difficult for them to deal with these feelings, when they are separated from their loved ones and their support network. It is easy for some people to say that prisoners made their own beds and must lie in them, but, if offenders are expected to sort their lives out, it is essential that they are motivated to become productive and constructive members of the community after their release. Prisoners who are experiencing feelings of worthlessness may end up depressed and on medication. It may then be difficult for them to see any purpose to their lives

Mental illness is generally regarded as being of a different quality to personality disorder described in *Section 19* and other parts of this book, and in some instances it will justify a spell in hospital. It may be one of the reasons why someone committed an offence, why the went 'off the rails'. The estimated 30 per cent of prisoners with mental health issues may find confinement particularly challenging. It is common for people who are locked away in an institution, for whatever reason, to feel that they have failed and been rejected by society; if they are in a poor state of mind, whether through mental illness or trauma, these feelings may be magnified.

Some believe that as these people will normally and eventually one day be released back into the community, it is in the best interests of society to build support systems, to make and maintain community links, however tentative, from the outside with prisoners, so that their eventual transition back into the community is likely to be a more successful one.

40 Some Useful Addresses

Assisted Prison Visits Unit
PO Box 2152, Birmingham, West Midlands
Tel: 0845 300 1423

Criminal Injuries Compensation Authority
Tay House, 300 Bath Street, Glasgow G2 4JR

Criminal Cases Review Commission
Alpha Tower, Suffolk Street, Queensway, Birmingham
B1 1TT

Commission for Racial Equality
Elliott House, 10-12 Allington Street, London
SW1E 5EH

Disability Rights Commission
Freepost MID 02164, Stratford upon Avon, Warwickshire

Liberty
21 Tabard Street, London SE1 4LA
Tel: 0207 403 3888

Lifer Review and Recall Section
Abell House, John Islip Street, London SW1P 4LH

Ministry of Justice
Selborne House, 54 Victoria Street, London
SW1E 6QW

Parole Board
Grenadier House, 99-105 Horseferry Road, London
SW1P 2DD

Prison and Probation Ombudsman
Ashley House, 2 Monck Street, London SW1P 2BQ

Prisoners' Advice Service
PO Box 46199, London EC1M 4XA

41 Prison Slang

Bacon	Sex offender
Bang-up	Time-in-cell
Block	A prison's punishment/segregation block
Burn	Tobacco
Doing bird	Serving a prison sentence
Double Bubble	Tobacco borrowed: double paid back
Cons	Prisoners (i.e. short for 'convicts')
Down the seg/block	In the block (above)
Draw	Cannabis
Gear/Brown	Heroin
Getting lifed-off	Getting a life-sentence
Getting knocked back	Refused parole/other 'bad news'
Getting spun	Having your cell searched
Grass	Informer
IEP Warning	IEPS privilege level could be reviewed
Jimmy (Boyle)	Tin foil (on which to chase heroin)
Joey	Small wrap of heroin
Keep your head down	Don't attract the attention of staff
L-plates	Life-sentence
Niki Lauda (powder)	Heroin
Nonce	Sex offender
On basic	On Basic IEPS privilege level (see *Section 1*)
On enhanced	On Enhanced IEPS privilege level
On meth	On methadone (a substitute for hard drugs)
On standard	On standard IEPS privilege level

On the gear	Heroin user
On the numbers	On protection
Pad	Cell
Puff	Cannabis
Rattling/clucking	Withdrawing from heroin, especially
Rock	Crack cocaine
Rub down	Body search by 'rubbing' hands down the body
Screw	Prison officer
Skins	Cigarette papers
Spin	A cell search
Three'd up	Three prisoners to a cell
Two'd up	Two prisoners to a cell
Two's up	Sharing a cigarette or roll-up
Weed	Cannabis

Index

A
absconding *36*
addresses *125*
adjudications *93*
advice *82, 85, 86, 121*
aggression *xvii, 54, 77, 94*
AIDS *79, 82*
anger *xvi, xxiii, 27, 116*
antisocial prisoners *35, 77*
appeal *110*
artificial insemination *95*
assessment *73*
avoiding 'sticking out' *77*

B
bank account *85*
bereavement *121*
bitterness *xvi*
bullying *xxiii, 55, 77, 78*

C
CALM *44*
CARATS *82*
care *41*
cells
  cellular confinement *94*
  occupancy of cells *39*
  shared cells *77, 80*
  strip cell *94*
challenging behaviour, etc. *49*
change
  desire to change *115*
chaos *xvi*
chaplains *90*
children *59*
  childhood *49*
choice
  positive choices *xvii*
Classroom Support Mentor *56*
closed conditions *35*
Cognitive Behaviour Therapy *73*
communication *54*
complaints *78, 97, 99*
  ombudsman to *100*
condoms *79*
confidence *xvi*
confidentiality *53, 82*

129

conflict *39*
  avoiding conflict *75*
confusion *27*
consequences *74*
control *77*
  controlling anger *116*
  controlling drug use *83*
  controlling others *77*
  volumetric control *117*
coping *36*
counselling *114*
Court of Appeal *43, 109, 110*
  reference to the court *107*
credit for a guilty plea *43*
Criminal Cases Review Commission *107*
criminal history *45*
Criminal Injuries Compensation Authority *105*
culture *xviii*

D

damage *xviii, 49*
dangerousness *xxiv, 36, 74*
  dangerous and severe personality disorder *73*
Data Protection Act *104*
deception *74*
degradation *xv*
denial *43*

depression *27, 83*
deprivation
  daily grind of deprivation *xiv*
despair *xvi, xxiii, 27*
deviancy *80*
difference *77*
disability *30, 61*
discharge *xviii, 35*
discrimination *56, 101*
disease *79*
diversity
  Diversity Representative *56*
dread *xvi*
driving lessons *69*
drugs *xvii, 28, 35, 62, 77, 81*
  drugs tests *36*
dysfunctionality *xvii*
dyslexia *55*

E

education *xviii, 29, 45, 77*
  positive learning experiences *xiv*
embarrassment *43*
emotions *27*
empathy *xvi, xxv, 73, 78*
enhanced thinking skills (ETS) *44*
escape *28*
ethics *xvi, 50*

European Court of Human Rights *32*, *93*, *95*, *109*
evil *78*
extortion *77*
'extra days' *94*

F
fairness *34*
family *xv*, *xxiv*, *27*, *39*, *59*, *66*, *100*
  dysfunctional family *xvii*
  family days *59*
fear *xvi*, *xxiii*
feelings *xvi*, *27*
firearms *28*
forgiveness *xxiii*
friends *66*
frustration *xix*

G
gender *56*
gossip *75*
'grass' *75*
grievances *54*
gross indecency *79*
guidance *xiii*

H
healthcare *27*, *79*
  medical file *103*

help
  asking for help *40*, *41*
hepatitis *79*
High Court *109*
HM Prison Blantyre House, *29*
HM Prison Dovegate *50*
HM Prison Grendon *49*
'homework' *31*
homosexuality *77*
honesty *82*
hopelessness *xxiii*
hospital
  secure hospital *73*
hostels *62*, *65*
humanity *xxi*
  inhumane acts *83*
humiliation *xv*
hurt *74*
hygiene *91*

I
impulse *74*
Incentives and Earned Privileges Scheme *28*
Independent Monitoring Board *94*, *100*
indeterminate sentences *xviii*, *109*
infection *79*, *91*
innocence *43*

Insiders *46*, *56*
Inside Time *xxi*
insight *xvi*, *74*
institutionalisation *xv*, *37*
interviews *73*
intimidation *77*
IQ tests *74*
isolation *39*

J
judicial review *34*, *109*

L
learning *xxiii*
  learning difficulties *61*
leave
  temporary leave *65*
legal aid *109*, *110*
licence *65*, *71*
  licence conditions *62*
  temporary licence *65*
lies *73*, *79*
life imprisonment *xxiv*
  lifer manager *61*, *86*
  lifer representative *xxi*
  mandatory lifers *67*
Listeners *27*, *46*, *53*, *80*, *90*
literacy *55*
loneliness *xvi*, *39*, *81*

M
manipulation *73*, *74*, *75*
manslaughter *28*
maturity *41*, *53*
media *xv*, *32*
meetings *54*
Members of Parliament *100*
mental health *xv*, *29*, *87*
  mental stability *xix*
mentoring *55*, *56*
Ministry of Justice *109*
miscarriages of justice *43*
mobile phones banned *63*
money management *85*
monitoring *35*
morale *xv*
morality *xvi*, *50*
motivation *115*

N
nonces *127*

O
obeying rules *36*
observation *35*
Offender Assessment System (OASys) *45*

INDEX

offender management
 Offender Management Unit (OMU) *47*
 offender managers *29, 35, 45*
offending behaviour courses *xxiii, 28, 35, 40, 44, 45, 74, 113*
official files *101, 103*
Official Secrets Act *28*
ombudsman *100*
open conditions *35, 61, 69, 85*
open-mindedness *115*
outside
 challenge of life outside *36*

P

pain *xiii, xxiii, 49, 75*
paperwork *33*
parole *xix, 29, 33, 35, 39, 47, 61, 67, 114*
 Parole Board *51*
 representations to *67*
permissions *71*
personal concerns *40*
personality disorder *73, 114*
 dangerous and severe personality disorder *73*
personal officer *40*
 Personal Officer Scheme *47*

police *99*
 calling in the police *94*
politics *75*
positive change *115*
possessions *117*
prejudice *56*
pressures *xiii*
priorities *xiii*
prison *xiii*
 community life in prison *35*
 HM Prison Service *45*
 long-term imprisonment *xv*
 open prison *29*
 Prison Rules *93*
 prison savings account *85*
prisoner
 life-sentence prisoner *27, 61, 67*
 prisoner categories *28*
 Prisoner Consultative Committee *54*
privileges *xvii, 55, 78, 94*
Probation Service *45, 61, 103*
 probation officers *71*
problems *xviii*
professionalism *41*
protection *55*
 protecting the public *67*
psychodrama *49*

psychology *ix, 29, 44, 61, 73, 74, 103*
   psychometric tests *73*
psychopathy *73, 74*
public interest *35*
punishment *xiv, 31*
purpose *viii*

Q
qualifications *ix*

R
race *101*
   racism *56*
rape *28*
Read and Grow *55*
Reasoning and Rehabilitation *116*
recall *67*
   reason for *68*
records *93*
rehabilitation *xxi*
reintegration into society *66*
relationships *39*
   race relations *101*
   relations liaison officer *101*
   same sex relationships *79*
   working at relationships *41*
release *xv, 31, 34, 35, 61*
religion *75*

remand *27*
remorse *27, 43, 74*
reports *44, 47, 73, 81*
   progress reports *40*
resettlement *29, 35, 62, 63, 65*
respect *xvii*
   respectful behaviour *40*
responsibility *viii, xiv, xviii, xxiv, 54, 120*
restorative justice *xv*
   restorative principles, etc. *xiv*
retribution *xxv*
review *33*
risk *xv, 29, 31, 36, 45, 51, 62, 67, 73, 115*
   high risk *39*
   manageable risk *36*
   prediction of risk/re-offending *74*
robbery *28*
role models *53*
rumour *76*
ruthlessness *73*

S
sabotage *36*
safety *40*
Samaritans *27, 53, 90*
sanitation
   in-cell sanitation *xvii*

INDEX

scalding *xxiv*
scars *xix*
Secretary of State *67*
segregation *ix, 94*
  segregation unit *75, 93*
self-confidence *54, 77*
self-esteem *xvi, 77*
self-harm *xvi, 89*
selfishness *xxiii*
sentence *xviii, 27*
  life-sentence *27, 29, 31*
  sentence plan *29, 40, 62, 113*
seriousness *45*
shame *xxiii, 27, 43, 89*
shock *27*
skills *xxiii, 29*
  social skills *39*
slang *127*
solicitors *32, 68, 97, 103, 109*
stages of a sentence *29*
Strangeways Riot *xvi*
stress
  stressful situations *39*
strip cell *94*
suicide *xxiv*
support *27, 35, 124*
survival *xiii, xxiv*

T
taboos *79*

talents *viii, 53*
targets *40*
tariff *29, 30, 31, 61*
  appeal against *30, 32*
  whole life tariff *32*
terror *xix*
terrorism *28*
therapy *49, 51*
  cognitive behaviour therapy *73*
  therapeutic communities *49*
thoughtlessness *xxiii*
tobacco *77*
Toe-by-Toe *55*
trainers *77*
training *ix*
trans-sexuals *77*
  transphobia *56*
trauma *xix, 49, 79*
treatment *xv, 27*
trust *28, 40, 73, 75, 90*

U
untreatability *73*

V
victims *xv, xx, xxiii, 73*
  victimisation *55*

violence *xvii, xxiv, 45, 78, 105*
   violence reduction *78*
   violence Reduction wing representative *46*
violin *vii*
visits *59*
   Assisted Prison Visits Unit *59*
   town visit *37*
volumetric control *117*
vulnerable prisoners *xvii, xviii*

W

warnings *36, 62, 127*
weakness *77*
Wing Representative *54*
work *53*
   community work *65, 85*
   voluntary work *46*
   work history *45*
   work placements *30*

ALSO FROM WATERSIDE PRESS

The Little Book of Prison: A Beginners Guide
by Frankie Owens

Koestler Platinum Award Winner. "Society wants to know about prison life, an interesting place to visit but you wouldn't want to live there".

- An easy-to-read prison survival guide of do's and don'ts.
- Perfect for anyone facing trial for an offence that may lead to imprisonment, their families and friends
- Packed with humour as well as more serious items
- Backed by prisoner support organizations

'By the end of the book, I felt like Frankie Owens was my cell-mate. His style and execution is either perversely skilful or an absolute fluke, but whatever it is, it is certainly good': *Prison Service Journal*.

Paperback | ISBN 978-1-904380-83-2 | February 2012 | 112 pages

Her Majesty's Philosophers by Alan Smith

Building on his *Guardian* pieces about teaching Philosophy in prison, this is Alan Smith's account *in extenso*. It is packed with insights and unexpected turns. It paints a picture in which worlds collide and conventional morality is turned inside out as 'new modes of discourse' change the men's thinking and ideas. At times surreal the book brings fresh perspectives to the minutiae of prison life: survival, coping, soap, teabags, cell mates, the constant noise and immediacy. And needless to say, the men come up with philosophical gems of their own.

Paperback | ISBN 978-1-904380-95-5 | September 2013 | 216 pages